Revelation, Inspiration, Scripture

LAYMAN'S LIBRARY OF CHRISTIAN DOCTRINE

Revelation, Inspiration, Scripture

JOHN M. LEWIS

BROADMAN PRESS
Nashville, Tennessee

© Copyright 1985 ● Broadman Press

All rights reserved

4216-33

ISBN: 0-8054-1633-1

Dewey Decimal Classification: 220.1

Subject Headings: BIBLE - INSPIRATION // REVELATION

Library of Congress Catalog Card Number: 83-71822

Printed in the United States of America

Library of Congress Cataloging in Publication Data

Lewis, John M., 1921-
  Revelation, inspiration, Scripture.

  (Layman's library of Christian doctrine ; v. 3)
  Includes index.
    1. Revelation. 2. Bible—Inspiration. 3. Bible—
  Evidences, authority, etc. 4. Bible—Canon.
  5. Theology, Doctrinal—Popular works. 6. Baptists—
  Doctrines. I. Title. II. Series.
  BT127.2.L45   1985   220.1   83-71822
  ISBN 0-8054-1633-1

To my wife,

Jean,

A special gift

of God's love and grace

Foreword

The *Layman's Library of Christian Doctrine* in sixteen volumes covers the major doctrines of the Christian faith.

To meet the needs of the lay reader, the *Library* is written in a popular style. Headings are used in each volume to help the reader understand which part of the doctrine is being dealt with. Technical terms, if necessary to the discussion, will be clearly defined.

The need for this series is evident. Christians need to have a theology of their own, not one handed to them by someone else. The *Library* is written to help readers evaluate and form their own beliefs based on the Bible and on clear and persuasive statements of historic Christian positions. The aim of the series is to help laymen hammer out their own personal theology.

The books range in size from 140 pages to 168 pages. Each volume deals with a major part of Christian doctrine. Although some overlap is unavoidable, each volume will stand on its own. A set of the sixteen-volume series will give a person a complete look at the major doctrines of the Christian church.

Each volume is personalized by its author. The author will show the vitality of Christian doctrines and their meaning for everyday life. Strong and fresh illustrations will hold the interest of the reader. At times the personal faith of the authors will be seen in illustrations from their own Christian pilgrimage.

Not all laymen are aware they are theologians. Many may believe they know nothing of theology. However, every person believes something. This series helps the layman to understand what he believes and to be able to be "prepared to make a defense to anyone who calls him to account for the hope that is in him" (1 Pet. 3:15, RSV).

Contents

1
Revelation as God's Self-Disclosure

The Divine/Human Encounter

How do we know God? How do we know what He is like? Can God's existence be proved by science? Can we by reason alone attain true knowledge of God? With so many conflicting ideas about God, how can we "test the spirits to see whether they are of God?" (1 John 4:1).

How are we to understand human religious nature? Why have there been so many religions in the course of history? Are the sacred writings of the world's varied religions of equal value? How do we relate the Christian faith to all other faiths? What is unique about Christian faith? How is it like and unlike other religions? Is there a common element to be found in all religions?

What about the Bible? Where did it come from? Who wrote it? What are its distinctive teachings? What does it have to say about God, man, religion, the world, history, and human destiny? How is it like and unlike other sacred writings? How are we to interpret the Bible? Why do we call the Bible the Word of God? Written in faraway lands centuries ago, in a language not our own, how does the Bible speak to us in our time, our language, our culture? Why do we claim a unique authority for the Bible? How do we test its truth? What is its unique message of salvation? Did God really inspire its writing? Where does Jesus Christ come into the picture?

In all the literature of the world, no other book has been more thoroughly examined than the Bible. It has withstood the most severe attacks of its enemies; yet it stands. It has guided and comforted untold multitudes through the centuries, making God real to them.

11

It continues to speak with persuasive authority to humanity in all walks of life, the rich and the poor, the learned and unlearned, the mighty and the downtrodden, among all nations, tongues, and cultures. The Bible makes good its unique claims over and over again to all who listen and respond in obedient faith to its message. It helps us understand ourselves—who we are, where we came from, and what kind of life we are to live. It helps us understand our unique place in the universe. No other book deals so honestly and fully with our spiritual and moral problems, our brokenness and sin, our anxieties and fears, our need for redemption.

The Bible presents us with a most exalted understanding of God's true nature as Creator, Judge, and Redeemer. It shows us our true nature. It presents a unique understanding of salvation for us as individuals, of the meaning of human history, and of the ultimate purpose in all creation. No other book speaks so clearly about our ultimate destiny.

The central claim of the Bible itself is that it preserves for us God's special revelation of Himself. That's how we know God, who He is, what He is like, and what He requires of us. As revelation it was not our discovery. It can neither be proved nor disproved by human reason, philosophy, or science. But by faith-obedience its claim can be verified in anyone's life who will listen and respond with an open mind, a prayerful heart, and a surrendered will.

The Bible presents history as His-story, an account of God's encounter with humankind. The Old Testament begins with an account of the creation—how all things began. It does not claim to be a scientific description. Its purpose is theological, to ground the created order in the sovereign, free, loving will of God. It tells us the who and why of creation, not the how and what. The climax of the account is the creation of humankind, both male and female made in God's image, endowed with God-given capacities whereby we are to live in communion with God, in fellowship with one another, and become colaborers with Him in the completion of His purpose in creation.

The awesome and tragic account of human rebellion is next presented as the source of man's sin and evil. The rest of the Old Testament recounts God's mighty deeds to redeem the human race. As the chosen vessel of God's redeeming grace, Israel's history is the record of God's preparatory revelation looking forward to the supreme revelation in the life, death, and resurrection of Jesus Christ.

In Jesus Christ the divine/human encounter reached its climax. In Him the Word of God—the power by which God created the world and through which He reveals himself—became flesh. The Gospels recount the life of Christ, His atoning death, and His triumphant resurrection as God's clearest, fullest, and final revelation of Himself to the world. The rest of the New Testament preserves the account of how the apostles, in obedience to Christ's command, went forth with the message of God's redeeming grace into all the world.

Thus the Bible is the record of God's self-disclosure in creation and redemption. It tells us we can know God because God has revealed Himself in the events and lives of those who composed the community of faith in Israel and the church. To know the history of the Bible, its nature and purpose, its truth and message is to be drawn into one's own encounter with the living God and so by faith to receive His great salvation.

Man's Longing to Know God

The widespread reality of religion.—Religious beliefs, rituals, customs, and relics are to be found in every civilization and culture. Human beings are incurably religious. If we understand what the Bible reveals to us about God's purpose in creation and how we fit into God's great scheme of things, we can also understand why we are religious beings. It helps us to understand the universal phenomenon of religion. Made in God's image we are endowed with "response-ability." We are made for fellowship and communion with God our Creator. Our true nature is to live lives of continuing companionship and obedient cooperation with God in fulfilling His purpose in creation. We cannot escape this deepest aspect of our nature. Augustine's great insight is a universal reality wherever human beings are found, "Thou madest us for Thyself, and our heart is restless, until it repose in Thee."

But the Bible makes another truth equally known to us about ourselves. Sin has entered into the situation. Our whole nature becomes twisted, distorted, and damaged so that we cannot now know God by our own unaided efforts. Yet the hunger for the true God remains alive and active in the human heart. Tragically it turns into idolatry. Luther summarized this viewpoint of the Bible with a grand simplicity, "Man either worships God or an idol."

In this Luther echoed faithfully the strict monotheistic view of the

Bible. In the inspired words of Isaiah we read, "Ye are my witnesses, saith the Lord, and my servant whom I have chosen: that ye may know and believe me, and understand that I am he: before me there was no God formed, neither shall there be after me" (43:10 KJV). And again, "Thus saith the Lord the King of Israel, and his redeemer the Lord of hosts; I am the first, and I am the last; and beside me there is no God" (44:6, KJV).

Throughout the writings of the prophets, God is spoken of as "the living God," in contrast to idols who can neither hear, nor speak, nor move. In Isaiah 44:9-20, the prophet described the plaintive absurdity of idol worship. A man cuts down a tree, builds a fire to cook his meals, and with the rest of the tree carefully fashions an idol before whom he then bows down in prayer, calling upon the idol to deliver him.

The inadequacy of man-made religion.—In the course of history almost every known object has been deified—mountains, rivers, trees, stars and planets, stones, animals, kings, heroes, and heavenly spirits. The varied and complex expressions of religions range "from primitive conceptions of dependence on powers and forces in the immediate social and natural environment to conceptions in the high religions of a first cause of all things, a being personal or impersonal that has produced the universe and is the present basis of its existence and functioning. In either case the religions, as a general rule, relate men closely with the power or powers at work in Nature and Society."[1] Nature and society are thought to be channels of the mysterious power behind all reality.

In the twin disciplines of comparative religion and the philosophy of religion, scholars have sought to analyze the origin, essence, and meaning of religion as such. Essentially, religion has to do with our understanding of the nature of the divine Being, how we are to be related to deity and how, then, we are compelled to live our lives according to the divine will. Present in all religious thought also is mankind's understanding of the world, its origin and meaning. Religion exhibits a vast variety of rituals, forms of worship, and ethical concepts. The variety is so extensive and complex as to defy any coherent or uniform description.

Part of the quest has been to find those elements present in all religions, of which any particular religion is but a peculiar example of the essentials. This approach assumes, to some degree, that all religions at bottom are the same. But so divergent are the concepts of God, or the gods, and humanity's place in the universe that it is obvious that all cannot be true at the same time. The task, therefore, of separating the true from the false becomes a central issue in the study of religion. And the core of this issue is our understanding of the reality and nature of the Divine Being.

What can serve as our point of reference for determining the true from the false? In this respect the Bible is unique. It makes the paramount claim that its content is the result of the self-revelation of the one and only true and living God. It sets this claim of unique revelation over against all other religions. Yet it recognizes the broken fragments of light that may be found there. Its description of our unique nature as made in the image of God helps us to understand why there are so many different religions in the course of human history. It is sympathetic to the longing in man's heart for the true and living God. It is equally emphatic that all other religions fall short of the mark of satisfying man's longing. There is a God-shaped question mark in the human heart that only God in Christ as recorded in the Bible can fill. The inadequacy of man-made religion is underscored throughout its sacred pages.

God's Longing for Man

Man's longing for God is balanced in Scripture with God's longing for man. Despite our sin, rebellion, and wayward wanderings, God has not given up on the human race. The Bible, therefore, is the account of God's undiminished love for us and His mighty acts of redeeming grace.

The moving lines of William Herbert Carruth set forth the universal human situation:

> Like tides on a crescent sea-beach,
>   When the moon is new and thin,
> Into our hearts high yearnings
>   Come welling and surging in;
> Come from the mystic ocean,
>   Whose rim no foot has trod,—
> Some of us call it Longing,
>   And others call it God.[2]

In actuality, the Bible reminds us that the human situation involves both man's longing for God and God's longing for man.

The necessity of revelation.—"Revelation literally means an unveiling, the lifting of an obscuring veil, so as to disclose something that was formerly hidden."[3] Zophar's question addressed to Job sets forth the necessity of revelation if we are to know God, "Can you find out the deep things of God?/Can you find out the limit of the Almighty?" (Job 11:7). The clear answer of the Bible is that God can be known only if and when God chooses to make Himself known. As sovereign Lord of creation and history, God cannot be manipulated or forced by us to reveal Himself. God takes the initiative to make Himself known. He does so in the ways, times, and manners of His own choosing, as the author of Hebrews made plain, "In many and various ways God spoke of old to our fathers by the prophets; but in these last days he has spoken to us by a Son, whom he appointed heir of all things, through whom also he created the world" (1:1-2).

In some manner, revelation is claimed by all religions. One or more of the various means of revelation may be shared by the different religions: oracles, the casting of lots, divination from animals and birds, dreams, angels, visions, theophanies (a direct manifestation of the deity), through seers, ecstatics, prophets, and mystics. Most are to be found in the Old Testament and some in the New Testament.

The uniqueness of the biblical revelation.—The mere claim to be a revelation is not sufficient in itself to convince one of the truth of the claim. One must examine the content and purpose of the revelation. In this regard, the biblical revelation stands in contrast to all other claims of revelation. By its very nature, revelation means a special knowledge is imparted to us which we cannot achieve for ourselves. It comes from beyond ourselves. It is of God's doing and initiative. The mystery of the divine nature is disclosed. This is the first element of uniqueness in the biblical revelation of which note must be taken. In the Bible, God is not giving mere ideas *about* Himself. God *Himself* confronts us.

"The main claim of revelation is not that the human recipient is made aware, by a special method, of a set of truths about God, but the far more exciting claim that he is made aware of God himself."[4] Ideas, rational concepts, doctrines, and so-called eternal truths are all essential vehicles as necessary witnesses to the revelation God has made of Himself. But they are not the primary revelation itself. They are revelation only in a secondary or derivative sense. As Trueblood reminds us, "Revelation comes as a religious experience rather than as a merely intellectual one."[5] That is to say, the biblical witness to revelation comes out of a divine/human encounter that is prior to the spoken or written account, to use Brunner's graphic insight.[6]

The recovery of this understanding of biblical revelation is one of the happier developments in Christian theological studies in recent times. It is also a recovery of the Reformation insight of the meaning of "justification by faith"—that Christ Himself is the object of saving faith and not the dogmas of an authoritarian church—which itself was a recovery of a true biblical insight as well.

John Baillie's historical review of this change from faith in church dogma to personal faith in God as He comes to us in Jesus Christ in his, *The Idea of Revelation in Recent Thought,* is most instructive in this regard. His main thesis is plainly summarized when he says, "It is not enough to think of God as giving us information by communication, but that we must think of Him as giving Himself to us in communion. . . . It is that what is fundamentally revealed is God Himself, not propositions about God."[7]

Nowhere does the Bible say God revealed Himself by writing a book about Himself. What it does say is that He inspired those whom He took the initiative to encounter to accurately interpret the meaning of that encounter that others may also come to know Him. The Bible, therefore, becomes an indispensible, unique, and irreplaceable vehicle used of God continually to reveal Himself to others.

The whole concept of revelation as a divine/human encounter is based on the Bible's unique revelation that God is personal and absolute in the disclosure of Himself.[8] The biblical way of putting this is the constant refrain that God is a "living God" and that He is God alone. The importance which the Bible places on the name (and names) of God underscores in unique ways the personal nature of God. To know God's name is to know His nature, character, and purpose.

Another unique feature of the biblical revelation is to recognize that the self-disclosure of God took place in a community of faith, first in

Israel and later in the church. God called into being both communities. And the very act of creating these communities is itself a revealing act of God. But more of this later.

Another unique feature of the biblical revelation is the importance attached to the concept of the Word of God. Here a human analogy can help us understand how this concept underlines both God's personal nature and the necessity of revelation if we are truly to know God. James cannot know Bill unless Bill is willing to "reveal" himself to James. James may indeed get to know a lot of true facts about Bill, but he can never really know Bill except in a personal encounter and only if Bill opens himself up to James. And Bill does this best through meaningful words that disclose his innermost thoughts, feelings, moods, motives, and purposes of life, all of which may also explain a great deal about Bill's actions.

Another analogy would be like going into a cabinet shop to find there a beautiful piece of furniture. By examining it one can learn a lot *about* the *maker*—his skill, his sense of beauty. But that is not the same as meeting the cabinetmaker himself. There is much more about the craftsman the cabinet cannot reveal about him. That takes a personal encounter.

These analogies are apt but, of course, not exhaustive for understanding how and why God has revealed Himself to us. The revelation of person to person must take place in a personal encounter. And words are necessary and important vehicles of both communication and communion. But words are symbols pointing to realities beyond themselves. They can never be substitutes for the reality. At times they can only make us aware of deeper depths in the reality for which we have no words. Much of the language of the Bible serves this latter purpose. Human language is incapable of giving us an exhaustive and perfect knowledge of God. One of the paradoxes of revelation is that God has revealed Himself clearly enough for us to really know Him but that He remains still shrouded in mystery.

Though revealed, God remains hidden to the eye of flesh. This hiddenness of God is also presented to us as a paradox in the Bible. At the dedication of the first Temple Solomon said, "The Lord has set the sun in the heavens, but has said that he would dwell in thick darkness" (1 Kings 8:12). Darkness is often used in Scripture as a metaphor of God's inaccessibility to us. It symbolizes also the lack of the knowledge of the true God in one's heart. It reminds us that, despite what God has revealed of His nature and purpose, there remains much about God we are incapable of knowing in the limitations of our mortality.

The ineffable glory of God's inner being is also spoken of as dwelling in light unapproachable by us. The apostle wrote to Timothy of God as the "only Sovereign, the King of kings and Lord of lords, who alone has immortality and dwells in unapproachable light, whom no man has ever seen" (1 Tim. 6:15-16). At the same time, light is a synonym for revelation.

The hidden God who nevertheless is revealed is variously stated in the biblical witness. Though known by us in His self-disclosure, there is a depth of the unknowable about God that can only evoke our response of awe, wonder, and humility before Him. This paradox is graphically set forth in the account of Moses' encounter with God recorded in Exodus 33:18-23.

> Moses said, "I pray thee, show me thy glory." And he said, "I will make all my goodness pass before you, and will proclaim before you my name 'The Lord'; and I will be gracious to whom I will be gracious, and will show mercy on whom I will show mercy. But," he said, "you cannot see my face; for man shall not see me and live." And the Lord said, "Behold, there is a place by me where you shall stand upon the rock; and while my glory passes by I will put you in a cleft of the rock, and I will cover you with my hand until I have passed by; then I will take away my hand, and you shall see my back; but my face shall not be seen."

Here is a genuine encounter with the living God, an awareness of His presence (v. 15), but not in ways of prescribing beforehand how He shall reveal Himself. We see His "back," after He has acted in a revealing event. His face remains hidden, symbol of the limits of our knowability. Yet He is truly known as we look back on His revealing acts. He acts first, then we know. He remains sovereign over all the ways He chooses to reveal Himself. But always at hand is the inspired interpreter to whom God has disclosed the meaning and content of the revealing encounter.

Hans Küng in his monumental and incisive work *Does God Exist?* finds Moses' encounter to be descriptive throughout Scripture of

God's revealing acts.[9] We can know who God is by what He has done in creation and redemption. We know Him in His passing by (v. 23).

The purpose of biblical revelation is also one of the Bible's distinctive characteristics. It is aimed at our redemption. While other religions set forth some scheme of redemption, the biblical concern is to restore God's image in us and to bring us back into a right relationship with God. The God who confronts us in the Bible is none other than the Creator Himself, who is sovereign Lord over nature and history.

Unlike other faiths, the biblical revelation is concerned for all humanity. God seeks the redemption of His children everywhere. The missionary imperative of the communities of faith, Israel and the church through whom the revelation has been given, becomes itself the continuing channel by which God makes Himself known. Those who receive the revelation are to share it with all the world.

The purpose of the Creator God is set forth by Isaiah 42:5-6:

> Thus says God, the Lord,
>   who created the heavens and stretched them out,
>   who spread forth the earth and what comes from it,
> who gives breath to the people upon it
>   and spirit to those who walk in it:
> "I am the Lord, I have called you in righteousness,
>   I have taken you by the hand and kept you;
> I have given you as a covenant to the people,
>   a light to the nations."

The prophets of Israel were constantly calling the Chosen People back to this divine commission. The New Testament, in which the revelation of God reaches its grand fulfillment, makes even plainer the intention of God in revelation to seek the redemption of all humankind. Jesus Christ is both God's supreme revelation of Himself and God's special deed of redeeming grace. He is now the message to be proclaimed.

Revelation as Encounter

Revelation as event.—We speak of the biblical revelation as historical. The revelation takes place in the sphere of human historical existence. It is God's personal disclosure of Himself to those chosen by Him to receive the revelation. As such it is a personal encounter in the ongoing flow of the history of people with whom He has established a covenant relationship. He makes His presence known to them in the ordinary and extraordinary events of their earthly pilgrimage.

The Bible's unique concept of history is essential for also understanding the nature of biblical revelation. God is revealed as the Lord of history. Pagan religions understand history as merely an extension of the cycles of nature. The Bible declares "that it is God who in His divine sovereignty writes history, allowing for the contingencies of Nature and the decisions of man, and weaving all in their partial meanings into the coherent pattern of His sovereign purpose. Thus the meaning of history must be sought in the nature and the purpose of God."[10]

In the Bible, history has a beginning, a direction, and an end. It is going somewhere. Since God is Lord, all nature and history reveal His purpose. But the clue to understanding comes in those special divine acts and events in which God reveals Himself and His purpose. The Bible is the inspired account of the meaning of those revealing events. The biblical revelation arises out of datable times and definite places among a particular people through specific interpreters.

Revelation as history divinely interpreted.—Revelation is not complete until someone receives God's interpretation and understands it as such. The biblical writers were not concerned merely to record the general occurrences of history. They were concerned only with those special events in which God made Himself known. These special events when linked together give a running account of God's redemptive purpose, as it unfolds across the centuries. So gaps in terms of general history occur throughout the account. The early chapters of Genesis, for example, are not meant to be an exhaustive record of chronological history. The writer touched only on the high spots of redemptive revelation. With this as our clue, we no longer need to worry about where Cain got his wife. The writer of Samuel and Kings often referred readers to the royal archives if they wanted to know more about certain kings in Israel. While the prophetic writings deal with historical events in the life of Israel, they do not assume to tell us everything that was happening at the time. The same is true of the Gospel accounts of Jesus' own life.

What John said about Jesus' life may be applied to the Bible as a whole: "Now Jesus did many other signs in the presence of the disciples, which are not written in this book; but these are written that you may believe that Jesus is the Christ, the Son of God, and that believing you may have life in his name" (John 20:30-31). What the Bible claims to do is to record the essential events of God's revealing and redemptive acts in history.

But even those events taken alone are not revelation. They must be interpreted, and God is His own interpreter. This, basically, is what the Bible means by inspiration. So inspiration and revelation are two sides of the same coin, so to speak.

The Bible as divine revelation is the written witness to the divine/human encounter in which God has made Himself personally known. The event of the encounter, whether with an individual or with the nation as a whole, is the primary revelation. The Bible is a secondary indispensable revelation in written form. One must keep in mind that God Himself is revealed as the essential clue for interpreting the Record. The aim of the biblical revelation is to draw us into our own redeeming encounter with God. Thus the biblical accounts can be spoken of as "salvation history."

General Revelation and Special Revelation

Revelation and reason.—For a proper understanding of biblical revelation, it is important to take seriously the distinction between knowledge of God Himself, which He alone can reveal, and all other forms of knowledge. Endowed by God with a superior intellect, we can acquire much true knowledge about the world, about ourselves, and about human history in general. The vast store of such knowledge has been an accumulative process through the centuries. It is always subject to correction by later discoveries. Out of such knowledge, philosophers and theologians have conceived the classical proofs for the existence of God. As objects of human thought, such proofs may indeed point toward God but are not the same thing as meeting God in a personal encounter as described in the biblical witness to God's self-disclosure of Himself.

Knowledge about God acquired through philosophical speculation gave rise in Western culture to the distinction between general revelation and special revelation. It was held that our knowledge of God comes in two ways: through human reason unaided by divine inspiration and through the special inspired revelation contained in the witness of Scripture.

Belief in a general revelation is based on the proposition that "man has been so created by God that, by means of his reason, he can perceive God in his works."[11] In summary fashion, the philosophical arguments for God's existence are as follows:

The Cosmological Argument simply affirms that it is rational to assume that the universe had an originating cause. The Teleological Argument advances the thought that the orderliness of the universe suggests that the originating cause must possess intelligence and a directing will to explain this orderliness.

The Anthropological Argument, also known as the Moral Argument, claims that man's sense of moral law requires a Lawgiver and a Judge to explain man's sense of guilt when disobeying the moral law.

The Ontological Argument is based on man's ability to conceive the idea of perfection; since existence is a necessary attribute of perfection, a perfect Being must exist. The idea of perfection cannot arise out of imperfect and finite things. Therefore, a Perfect Being must be the source of the idea itself.[12]

These arguments do not really prove the existence of God. They only suggest that it is more rational than irrational to conclude God's possible existence. However, divinity so conceived falls short of the nature and purpose of God as set forth in the biblical record. Divinity so conceived does not suggest a personal encounter with God as necessary for actually knowing Him. Further, the concepts are stated in abstract terms devoid of the aliveness of God who meets us in Scripture. Nor do these abstractions take seriously man's need of redemption. They do not speak of God as one who cares about us or is seeking contact with us.

These abstract ideas do not conceive of God as seeking to create a community of faith wherein we are to live in a relationship of peace, justice, mercy, and mutual goodwill with our fellow human beings. They are vague as to what God's purpose for man is. They are equally vague as to our eternal destiny. They lack any concept of history as the arena of the divine activity.

Eventually such philosophical arguments can logically lead to pantheism (nature is God, God is nature), or Deism (God remote, unconcerned, unmoved by man's plight, the "Absentee God"), or, more tragically still, into atheism itself.

The Scriptures do not discount the proper place of reason for our understanding of God. It is insistent, however, that unaided by God's own revelation of Himself, reason cannot ultimately lead us to the truth of God. Indeed, God invites us to "reason together" (Isa. 1:18) with Him about His mighty acts of redemption on our behalf. Jesus reminded believers that we are to love God with our minds (Matt. 22:37). When redeemed, reason becomes a necessary and powerful endowment for knowing God as He has revealed Himself.

God knowledge versus world knowledge.—All forms of knowledge apart from the biblical revelation may be spoken of as world knowledge. It is knowledge which we acquire for ourselves about the world and all it contains. It does not come through direct revelation but through human discovery and scientific research. It falls in the category of "general revelation" inasmuch as all truth comes from God. But it is not to be equated with the God knowledge of the biblical revelation God has made of Himself. All world knowledge has come through a progressive accumulation through the centuries. The process has moved from primitive animism and the "myths of the gods," as in the polytheisms of ancient Babylon, Egypt, Greece, and Rome, to the sophistication of modern science.

All world knowledge, as distinct from God knowledge, is the result of our scientific research, experimentation, and application. While early man's world knowledge contained a great deal of true facts about nature, man, and history, it really was a mixed bag. Pagan myths, astrology, and rites of sympathetic magic were included in mankind's understanding of the world. The Greek nature philosphers were among the first to attempt to systematize human knowledge on the basis of the reality of matter.

In the Athenian school of Socrates and Plato, the concept that eternal ideas alone possessed reality and stood behind all sense perception soon guided both philosophy and science. Although he employed observation and experimentation, even Aristotle held to other popular ideas of his day. He believed that the earth was at the center of the universe with the heavenly bodies moving round it in ever-expanding cycles. Ptolemy, through his writings, passed this view into the thought of the Middle Ages.

The early fathers of the church, especially Augustine, sought to interpret the Scriptures in the light of the philosophy of Plato and Aristotle. In the thirteenth century, Thomas Aquinas built up a complete scheme of rational knowledge combining Christian doctrine with Aristotle's philosophy and science. Modern science had its beginnings with more sure methods of observation and experimentation during the Renaissance.

The deductive method begins with the eternal ideas believed to be in the human mind from birth. This method gave way to the inductive method. The inductive method begins with systematic observation of the facts of experience. So science proceeds as follows: observation serves as the base; a hypothesis is formulated to explain the facts; experimentation formulates a law of nature; and further testing confirms all conclusions. Finally all knowledge in a given area of investigation is systematized. But modern science still proceeds on the idea that the universe, and all it contains, yields to rational investigation, a legacy from the Greeks.

What has all this to do with our understanding of the Bible? Much in many ways. And so we proceed to examine this concern.

Revelation and science.—Our concern with the relationship of science to the biblical revelation is threefold: Why should we avoid confusing biblical revelation with the scientific views of any age? how can we oppose the view that science is the only method for acquiring truth? and how can we understand the Bible in the light of modern science?

The first concern came to a head when Copernicus, a Polish astronomer born in 1473, set forth the revolutionary idea that the sun did not move around the earth but that the earth revolved around the sun. With a newly improved telescope, Galileo proved Copernicus correct. Church leaders refused to look through the telescope, and the Church condemned both men as heretics.

Accepting the prescientific views of Plato, Aristotle, and Ptolemy as supposedly reflected in the Scriptures, the church continued to challenge the corrected views of modern science. On the basis of taking the chronology of Genesis as literal science, Lightfoot of Cambridge concluded the earth was created on October 23, 4004 BC at nine o'clock in the morning.[13] Bishop Usher (1580-1656) agreed, and the date was long printed in the margin of English Bibles. Luther and

Calvin denied the view of Copernicus and accepted Lightfoot's dating.[14] But research in geology, archaeology, paleontology, and astro-
physics now measure the age of the world and universe in billions of
years.

People of biblical times seem to have accepted the "three-story
view" of the world: the earth was flat; the solid dome of the firmament
overarched the earth; the underworld was beneath the earth. All this
was surrounded by mountain peaks and water. God dwelled in the
heavens above the firmament.[15] For the church to claim that such
prescientific views were part of the divine revelation was a tragic
mistake. Such a position obscured the true nature of revelation and
was a failure to understand the human element in the transmission of
the revelation.

As modern science continues to refine our world knowledge, in no
way does it invalidate the God knowledge of the Bible as God's
self-disclosure of Himself. As Paul reminded readers, "We have this
treasure in earthen vessels, to show that the transcendent power belongs to God and not to us" (2 Cor. 4:7).

The false conflict between the Bible and modern science came as the
result of the church of the Middle Ages misunderstanding the nature
of its own Scriptures and revelation. This should warn us of the error
of confusing biblical revelation with the scientific findings of any age.
The world knowledge acquired by science properly falls under the
category of general revelation. While serving as confirming evidence
of biblical revelation, it must never be equated with it.

Secondly, we must be concerned when science is considered the
only method for acquiring truth. The scientific method should be
confined to the study of the structure of the physical universe and its
dynamic energies, including the fields of biology, psychology, sociology, and history. When people use the scientific method to explain total
reality, they pass over into the arena of philosophy and theology.
Whenever this is done, the logical result is either Deism (the "absentee
God"), as in the Age of Reason, or atheism (God as a projection of
man's wishful desire), as with Freud, Feuerbach, Karl Marx, and
Nietzsche. It can also lead to some form of pantheism (nature is God,
God is nature), as in the teachings of Hegel or as in Far Eastern
religions.[16]

In no way can "scientism" prove or disprove the biblical truth of

God's own revelation of Himself. The Bible is in a category all its own. It deals with something unique—God's revelation of Himself. It will reflect honestly the limited world knowledge of its writers; it will resemble in many respects what we find in other man-made religions, but none of these elements are essential factors in the unique content of the biblical revelation. It arose out of the stuff of ordinary history through which God has acted. Its truth as revelation must be discerned in how it differs from human science and religions. We need to distinguish science from scientism. Science is the valid pursuit of knowledge through the inductive method. Scientism is the false assumption that science provides all knowledge and can solve all human problems.

Our third concern is a serious and necessary one for modern man. The advance of modern science may well be considered part of the divine purpose. God's commands in the creation accounts "to subdue the earth" and "till" the garden (Gen. 1:28; 2:15) may well be called a "theological mandate" for scientific research. The acquisition of world knowledge through our superior God-given intelligence is part of the meaning of having been created in God's image. We are placed here to exercise a kind of lordship over the earth, to fulfill a stewardship as God's tenants, as colaborers with him in fulfilling the divine purpose.

> What is man that thou art mindful of him,
> and the son of man that thou dost care for him?
> Yet thou hast made him little less than God,
> and dost crown him with glory and honor.
> Thou hast given him dominion over the works of thy hands;
> thou hast put all things under his feet.
>
> Psalm 8:4-6

The biblical revelation of man's nature does not center in his superior intellect. It centers in our capacity for fellowship with God. We have "response-ability." We are answerable to our Creator. How we acquire world knowledge (our science) is one thing. God is most concerned about how we use it. The truth of science and how we use it becomes, therefore, a moral issue. All truth is of God—we can discover only what God has already put into the order of creation. The universe responds to our rational powers. The biblical revelation would require that all our science serve to glorify God and serve human needs. As Paul put it, we are to "take every thought captive to obey Christ" (2 Cor. 10:5), for He who is the Truth is the clue to our proper understanding and use of all other forms of knowledge.

Notes

1. John B. Noss, *Man's Religions* (New York: The Macmillan Company, 1956), p. 3.

2. Roy J. Cook, ed., *One Hundred and One Famous Poems* (Chicago: Contemporary Books, Inc. 1958), p. 104

3. John Baillie, *The Idea of Revelation in Recent Thought* (New York: Columbia University Press, 1956), p. 19.

4. David Elton Trueblood, *Philosophy of Religion* (New York: Harper Brothers, 1957), p. 29.

5. Ibid.

6. Emil Brunner, *Truth as Encounter* (Philadelphia: The Westminster Press, 1964).

7. Baillie, p. 49.

8. Emil Brunner, *Revelation and Reason* (Philadelphia: The Westminster Press, 1946), p. 23

9. Hans Küng, *Does God Exist?* (New York: Doubleday and Company, Inc., 1980), p. 654.

10. E. C. Rust, *The Christian Understanding of History* (London: Lutterworth Press, 1947), p. 17.

11. Brunner, *Revelation and Reason,* p. 68.

12. Augustus Hopkins Strong, *Systematic Theology* (Philadelphia: The Judson Press, 1907), pp. 71-90.

13. Brunner, *Revelation and Reason,* p. 278.

14. Ibid.

15. Rust, p. 4

16. Küng, 129-425.

2
Revelation in the Old and New Testaments

The Old Testament: The Preparatory Revelation

Revelation in the Creation

Having first met Yahweh (the covenant name for God, explained more fully later in this chapter) in the Exodus deliverance as Redeemer, subsequent revelation made clear to Israel that, as the only true and living God, He was none other than the Creator of all things. Henceforth, Israel's literature makes frequent references to God as Lord of nature as well as Lord of history—all history. Unlike her pagan neighbors, Israel did not worship the moon and stars, or anything else in nature, although the literature reflects much lingering popular superstition until after the purging of the captivity. Israel had no concept of nature as a realm existing under the control of natural law. All was under the lordship of God. The created order, therefore, was equally the arena of God's immediate activity. So the psalmist could declare—"The heavens are telling the glory of God;/and the firmament proclaims his handiwork" (Ps. 19:1). From the viewpoint of biblical revelation the created order is a primary and universal revelation to all people everywhere.

The created order reveals the reality of God.—In writing to the Romans, Paul made special use of this biblical insight.

> Ever since the creation of the world his invisible nature, namely, his eternal power and deity, has been clearly perceived in the things that have been made. So they are without excuse (Rom. 1:20).

Thus the Bible affirms the possibility of a true knowledge of God available to any rational and discerning mind. In this regard, the

29

biblical revelation makes contact with the various philosophical arguments for God's existence.

The orderliness, beauty, complexities, and dynamic forces of nature point to a supreme intelligence of almighty power as the source and directing reality behind all things. We must remember, however, that Paul was speaking out of the context of the special revelation of the Old Testament. The created order is God's handiwork. It is a reality, with its own unique structure, that stands over against God. It is not to be confused with God Himself, as in pantheism.

The more exact knowledge of the world acquired by modern science confirms the biblical insight. For example, for supporting life, our planet is uniquely situated: it is located just the right distance from the sun, avoiding the extremes of cold and heat; it revolves about the sun tilted at twenty-three and a fraction degrees, making the change of seasons possible as it turns on its axis; it has an abundance of water, a rare element in the universe; and all living things are extremely complex. Speaking of the God who brought order out of chaos, Isaiah was inspired to comment—"he established it;/he did not create it a chaos,/he formed it to be inhabited!" (Isa. 45:18). Such precise order points to a supreme intelligence.

Our scientific technology points in the same direction. The Saturn 5 rocket contains over 15 million parts, 3 million as functioning parts. It was designed by over 400,000 men and women from 120 universities and laboratories and 20 industrial firms. The instrument panel has 24 instruments, 566 switches, and 71 signal lights. Before blast-off, 887,500 inspection points are checked in the countdown. In orbit, 40,000 people are on standby to help in case of trouble in flight. Numerous tracking stations are located worldwide to keep up with the rocket. The capsule in which the astronauts ride is carefully designed for all life-support systems. Complex computers on board aid in manning the spaceship. The space center in Texas is in constant touch by radio monitoring every second of the flight.

We know it took intelligence to marshal and coordinate this total system of knowledge and technology. Yet, any one of the billions of cells in the human body is more complex still. The most rational conclusion points to an even greater intelligence behind all the complexity of the universe, including the marvel of human intelligence and its accomplishments. The Greek philosophers were on the right track to discern an infinite Logos (reason, meaning, intelligence) as the ultimate reality resident in the created order. The British philosopher, Lord Balfour, made this perceptive statement—"We know too much about matter to be materialists."

But Paul's concern lay at a deeper level. He went on to say—

> For although they knew God they did not honor him as God or give thanks to him, but they became futile in their thinking and their senseless minds were darkened. Claiming to be wise, they became fools, and exchanged the glory of the immortal God for images resembling mortal man or birds or animals or reptiles (Rom. 1:21-23).

Throughout, the Bible takes into account humanity's sinfulness. Because of sin the general revelation in the created order turns into idolatry. Man's distorted response to this universal revelation is itself a clear sign of our sinfulness. From the biblical perspective, we can understand why there have been so many different religions. Speaking of the world outside the community of faith to whom a special revelation has been given, Paul said, "they exchanged the truth about God for a lie and worshiped and served the creature rather than the Creator, who is blessed forever" (Rom. 1:25).

Idolatry takes many forms: in the crude making of images, the pagan myths of the gods, or systems of human thought however highly developed. All stand as proud obstacles to the knowledge of God in biblical revelation (2 Cor. 10:5).

General revelation not sufficient for salvation.—Had man not sinned, the general revelation would have been adequate for living in loving and faithful obedience to the Creator. But once distorted into idolatry, a special revelation became necessary to redeem us. This special revelation occurs in the realm of history. God's chief concern is for the creatures He has made in His image for communion and fellowship with Him. While much about God can be discerned in the created order, He still remains the hidden God. The creation speaks of God's power but does not disclose His personal nature and purpose. It does not lead to a personal encounter with Him. That can occur only in the divine/human encounter of special revelation aimed at redeeming the sinner so he can then know God in all the ways of His revealing. Only from the viewpoint of the special revelation can we once again understand and appreciate the general revelation in creation.

Because God can be known in His general revelation, our distortion of it sits in judgment on us. So "the wrath of God is revealed from heaven against all ungodliness and wickedness of men who by their wickedness suppress the truth" (Rom. 1:18). The revelation of God in creation remains available to all. Our failure to understand God's revelation aright is the background against which the special revelation is cast. Without the special revelation, we continue to distort the general revelation and so remain under judgment.

Revelation and the First Covenant

The two great historical events in which the special revelation occurred are the redemptive deliverance of Israel from the bondage of Egypt, and the life, death, and resurrection of Jesus the Christ. The events are related to each other as promise and fulfillment. The unity of the Bible, composed of the sixty-six books of both Testaments, arises out of their consistent witness that it is the same God who alone is God, Creator, Judge, and Redeemer, who is making Himself known. But this unity must not be allowed to obscure the rich and varied ways in which the revelation took place.

God created a covenant people.—The central event of the Old Testament is the deliverance from Egypt and the founding of the covenant at Sinai. God's revelation of Himself to Moses provides us with the basic clue for understanding the nature of all special revelation. At the burning bush, God confronted Moses in a theophany (God's presence made real through some material means). In this divine/human encounter, God addressed Moses by name and revealed Himself as the God of Abraham, Isaac, and Jacob.

God then revealed His concern for His people in Egypt. He had heard their affliction and was ready to deliver them (Ex. 3:1-8). The sign of assurance given to Moses is to be seen in the historical act of the deliverance itself.

> But I will be with you; and this shall be the sign for you, that I have sent you: when you have brought forth the people out of Egypt, you shall serve God upon this mountain (Ex 3:12).

In the ancient world, deity was thought to show itself most powerfully in the dynamic forces of nature, in family, field, and flock. It was also believed that to know the name of a god gave one power to control the divine energies to some desired effect. So Moses asked for God's name as further assurance that Moses could achieve deliverance.

At this point in the encounter, God revealed His personal name to Moses. Herein lies the most distinctive feature of the biblical revelation—to know God's name is to know God as a personal being who seeks personal communion with us, uniquely endowed by our Creator with "response-ability." To speak of God as possessing a "name" is to speak of God's personality.

In the Bible, names are of great importance. A name conveys the unique character and nature of the person. God's personal name revealed to Moses—Yahweh—is often translated "I Am who I Am" (Ex. 3:14). Thus translated it can mean, "I am the living One." Another interpretation says it can mean, "I cause to be" or bring into being. It became for Israel the revelation that God is Lord of history. It signifies also that God possesses sufficient power to accomplish all His purposes. While called by many other names in the Old Testament, Yahweh remains the special name of redeeming grace.

Following the deliverance from Egypt, God established His special covenant with Israel at Sinai. Covenant agreements were widespread in that ancient world: between individuals (Gen. 21:7); between husband and wife (Mal. 2:14); between tribes (1 Sam. 11:1); between rulers (1 Kings 20:34); between a king and his subjects (2 Kings 11:4). Such covenants set forth the rights and duties of the respective parties. Yahweh's covenant with Israel was not between equals but reflected God's lordship over Israel as her Redeemer. This lordship is cited over and over again in the reminder that God had first acted in a redeeming event in history, namely the Egyptian deliverance.

At Sinai God instituted his special covenant with Israel.

> You have seen what I did to the Egyptians, and how I bore you on eagle's wings and brought you to myself. Now therefore, if you will obey my voice and keep my covenant, you shall be my own possession among all peoples; for all the earth is mine, and you shall be to me a kingdom of priests and a holy nation (Ex. 19:4-6).

The heart of the covenant is contained in the Ten Words of commandment, whose preamble also reminded Israel of her great deliverance from Egypt: "I am the Lord your God, who brought you out of . . . Egypt, out of the house of bondage" (Ex. 20:2).

All subsequent requirements of God were expanded into the Book of the Covenant (Ex. 20:22 to 23:33), and the Holiness Code (Lev. 17—26), along with a growing body of law dealing with religious and civil matters as well.

Israel was also conscious of God's providential guidance of her earlier ancestors. She traced her ancestry back to Abraham with whom God had also made a covenant agreement.

> Now the Lord said to Abram, "Go from your country and your kindred and your father's house to the land that I will show you. And I will make of you a great nation, and I will bless you, and make your name great, so that you will be a blessing. I will bless those who bless you, and him who curses you I will curse; and by you all the families of the earth shall bless themselves" (Gen. 12:1-3).

Through Abraham, from among the Semitic tribes, the Hebrews had their beginning. Abraham came late onto the stage of history. By then the world was old, as was religion and civilization. The Old Babylonian culture out of which he came was highly developed. Yet Israel was aware of the stream of history that stretched beyond Abraham. Through revelation, aware of God's concern for all mankind, Israel set her own history down in the context of world history. The proper beginning for relating God's use of Israel as His vehicle for reaching out to all the world was to place first, therefore, the revealed accounts of God's purpose in the creation narratives. Long before the covenant with Abraham, God's covenant with all humanity was recited in God's promise to Noah. "While the earth remains, seedtime and harvest, cold and heat, summer and winter, day and night, shall not cease" (Gen. 8:22).

The covenant at Sinai was the culmination of God's redeeming revelation to create a special community of faith through whom He was to reach out to all mankind. The history of Israel from Sinai onward is the outworking of that purpose until it was finalized and completed in the coming of Jesus as the Christ.

Moses' encounter with God, the deliverance from Egypt, the giving of the Ten Commandments, and the institution of the Sinai covenant make up the pivotal revelatory event of the Old Testament.

Looking backward to the very dawn of creation itself and moving forward with God in history, biblical revelation is grounded in the reality of the stuff of history. The giving of His name reveals God as personal in His dealings, as One who works through inspired interpreters in special revelatory events to complete His purpose of redemption. The biblical narratives do not give an exhaustive account of the chronological sweep of history in general. They concentrate on the revealing-redemptive events.

The life and culture of Israel resembled its neighbors in many respects. Social customs, religious rituals, elements of social and civic culture, language, the popular world knowledge of the day were all shared with others. What made Israel's life and culture links of revelatory historical events was her relation of all these matters to God's special purpose for and through Israel for all the world.

From God's promise through Abraham to bless all mankind, to Israel's commission at Sinai to be a "kingdom of priests," to the inspired insight of the great prophets that Israel was to be a "light to the nations," her history is His-story of redemptive revelation.

Israel's history may be likened to the Gulf Stream flowing through the Atlantic Ocean. In the Gulf Stream, the water is as wet and salty as the rest of the ocean (Israel is much like her neighbors in many respects). The difference is in the temperature and directional flow of the stream. God's providential, revelatory presence in Israel's history made the difference. He was moving all history through Israel's history to the completion of His purpose begun in creation.

God raised up the prophets.—The history of Israel from Sinai to the coming of Jesus is the account of Israel's obedience and disobedience to the covenant. Along with the giving of His name as signifying God's personal presence, the concept of the "Word of God," developed as the basic way for understanding biblical revelation. The Hebrew term *dabar* (pronounced da-var) has a wide range of meanings. It can stand for a thing, a situation (event), or as a word in ordinary speech. It often refers to the "acts of God" in which He reveals Himself. In a collective sense, it can refer to a message which contains many "words." In the later chapters of Isaiah, it is practically a synonym for God's revelation in history.[1]

In biblical revelation, God's *word* and *act* are two sides of the same coin. His word is an act, His act is a word. He has only to speak and His will is done.

Over the years, Israel developed an elaborate system of sacrifices by which the covenant was kept in force. An ordained line of priests administered the system. Sacrifices were provided and required for the offering of thanks and atonement for sin. The three great festival feasts required of Israel kept fresh in the minds of the celebrants God's redemptive acts in history. Passover recalled the deliverance from Egypt; Tabernacles, the feast of harvest, recalled God's providence in the wilderness wanderings; and Pentecost, the feast of ingathering, recalled the giving of the law at Sinai.

But it was through the word of the prophet that God continued to reveal His presence, judgment, and purpose to His chosen. The prophets spoke out of their contemporary situation God's continuing word of revelation and redemption. Sometimes it was a word of judgment as the prophets called Israel to repentance for breaking the covenant. It was also a word of mercy and forgiveness.

Earlier more primitive forms of the divine communication, such as divination, oracles, visions, and theophanies, eventually gave way to God's Word spoken through the prophets. "God gives to His Prophets the authentic interpretation of His revelation in history, which, without this interpretation, would remain more or less an insoluable enigma."[2]

The life, experiences, and words of the prophets are living witnesses to the nature of biblical revelation: in a genuine divine/human encounter God inspired His chosen spokesmen properly to interpret His presence in the covenant community through whom God was seeking the redemption of a fallen race. All occurs in the blood, sweat, and tears of the ordinary and extraordinary events of Israel's history as God led her forward to the supreme revelation in Jesus Christ.

One of the amazing things about the biblical revelation is how "the Word of God" is expressed in human words. God used the prophets' own vocabulary and thought patterns. They were part of the "earthen vessel" through which the revelation was communicated. The limitation of their world knowledge was not a hindrance to the revelation. Such matters were not part of the revelation itself, as the church of the Middle Ages misunderstood, but testify to the historical reality through which the revelation was given.

The "Word of God" was first God's revealing activity. It was then reported and witnessed to in the prophet's interpretation as inspired by God. The spoken words and later the written words of the prophets took on many forms, all pointing to the living God Himself. At times it is teaching about God, setting forth His commands and requirements: "Hear, O Israel: the Lord our God is one Lord; and you shall love the Lord your God with all your heart, and with all your soul, and with all your might. And these words which I command you this day shall be upon your heart" (Deut. 6:4).

At other times God's Word is heard in quite ordinary situations: Jeremiah watching the potter or Amos observing a basket of summer fruit. Often the prophet declared God's Word in an enacted parable: Jeremiah bearing a yoke on his shoulders (Jer. 28:10); Isaiah symbolizing God's judgment by walking about naked and barefoot (Isa. 20:2-3); or Ezekiel instructed to sketch besieged Jerusalem upon a broken tile (Ezek. 4:1-3).

More often God's Word came as an interpretation of some historical event in which God's judgment or redemption was being revealed. Even through one who did not know Him, God spoke a redeeming word of hope, as in the conquests of Cyrus (Isa. 45:1-5).

God communicated His presence through the many anthropomorphisms (God conceived in terms of human thoughts, emotions, traits, and actions) in the biblical record. None of them is to be taken in a crass and literal sense however. They are earthen speech that conveys God as a living, personal Presence. They are part of the rich and colorful vocabulary used by the prophets witnessing to the living God who acts redemptively on behalf of His people.

One such anthropomorphic expression is of special significance. We find it in the many references to the "face" of God. No other expression conveys the truth of a divine/human encounter as the central meaning of biblical revelation so graphically. To hide His face shows God's anger: "In overflowing wrath for a moment/I hid my face from you" (Isa. 54:8). Or it may be a display of God's love and grace: "The Lord make his face to shine upon you, and be gracious to you" (Num. 6:25). It signifies God's willingness to redeem His people: "For the

Lord your God is gracious and merciful, and will not turn away his face from you, if you return to him" (2 Chron. 30:9).

Therefore, the following are the basic catagories that help us best understand biblical revelation. God revealed Himself in the giving of His name. God revealed Himself in historical acts of divine judgment and redemption. The prophets used figures of speech such as "God's Word" and "God's Face" to reveal God Himself to the people. The concept of the covenant revealed God's relationship with the Hebrews.[3]

The basic content of the prophetic witness to God's self-disclosure has to do with making known God's moral character and the requirement that His people be conformed to His holiness, justice, and mercy.

The Hebrew word *qadosh* ("holy," "holiness") has the primary meaning of that which is separate and, therefore, refers to the unique nature of God as God alone. It refers to the depths of mystery in God and the total otherness of God. He alone is holy. It signifies the separation between the Creator and the creature. Rudolf Otto in his classic work, *The Idea of the Holy,* drawing on data from many religions, describes the holy as that attribute of God which evokes awe and reverence in the presence of God. In one form or another, it is found in the taboos of many religions. In Otto's thought, "The wholly other is the Holy Other." To ascribe holiness (deity) to any reality apart from its relationship to God and His exclusive use is idolatry.

The secondary meaning of holiness derives from the reality of God's moral perfection. It includes the ideas of purity and perfect goodness, also grounded in the nature of God as God alone. It stands in contrast to all that is corrupt or unclean. As the Holy God, He is also just, righteous, merciful, kind, and compassionate.

Isaiah reminded Israel over and over again that the Holy One had redeemed her, "For I am the Lord [Yahweh] your God, the Holy One of Israel, your Savior" (Isa. 43:3; also see 43:14-15; 48:17). Hosea spoke of "the Holy One in your midst" (Hos. 11:9), making plain that the transcendent God has made Himself known in Israel's history.

The main burden of Amos is on God's requirement that His people "let justice roll down like waters, and righteousness like an everflowing stream" (5:24). Burdened over Israel's idolatry, and out of his own tragic experience with Gomer, Hosea declared God's redemptive love and mercy for the faithless nation. Out of His righteous mercy, God called Israel to return to Him, "for the ways of the Lord are right,/ and the upright walk in them,/but transgressors stumble in them./ For I desire steadfast love and not sacrifice,/the knowledge of God, rather than burnt offerings" (14:9; 6:6).

The moral requirements of God are summarized in the classic statement of Micah 6:8:

> He has showed you, O man, what is good;
> and what does the Lord require of you
> but to do justice [Amos], and to love kindness
> [Hosea], and to walk humbly with your God? [Isaiah]

Combining ritual law and moral law, the Holiness Code (Lev. 17—26), likewise summarizes the insistence of the prophets that God requires conformity to His character as the purpose of His redeeming revelation:

> For I am the Lord your God; consecrate yourselves therefore, and be holy, for I am holy. . . . For I am the Lord who brought you up out of the land of Egypt, to be your God; you shall therefore be holy, for I am holy. You shall do no injustice in judgment. You shall not hate your brother in your heart. But you shall love your neighbor as yourself: I am the Lord (Lev. 11:44-45;19:15,17,18).

The high-water mark of the Old Testament revelation is to be seen in the ethical teachings of the great prophets of Israel. The unfolding revelation of God moved from the primitive polytheism of Israel's ancestors ("Your fathers lived of old beyond the Euphrates . . . and they served other gods" Josh. 24:2), through Israel's constant battle with idolatry, to the clear disclosure of pure monotheism. Hosea reminds us that it was through the inspired words of the prophets that God was able finally to reveal the truth about Himself:

> I spoke to the prophets;
>   it was I who multiplied visions,
> and through the prophets gave parables.
> By a prophet the Lord brought Israel up from Egypt
>   and by a prophet he was preserved (Hos. 12:10,13).

God promised the Messiah.—As it became apparent to the prophets that Israel was unable to keep the covenant, the hope of a future, final, and complete revelation of God arose in their preaching. The promise of this future revelation became an essential part of the Old Testament revelation itself.

Next to the Exodus deliverance, the Babylonian captivity became the second great event in Israel's history whereby her faith and hope were clarified. Again the inspired prophets helped Israel understand what was happening. The captivity did not mean God was weaker than the gods of the Babylonians. Rather it was a revelation of God's righteous judgment of His own people. Nor did it mean God had forsaken His purpose and His people. He would bring them back home and go on with His intention to provide redemption for all humanity.

The hope of future deliverance took on many forms. Isaiah reminded the nation that "a remnant will return, the remnant of Jacob, to the mighty God. For though your people Israel be as the sand of the sea, only a remnant of them will return. Destruction is decreed, overflowing with righteousness" (Isa. 10:21-22).

Ezekiel voiced God's promise in moving figures of speech:

> I myself will be the shepherd of my sheep, and I will make them lie down, says the Lord God. I will seek the lost and I will bring back the strayed, and I will bind up the crippled, and I will strengthen the weak, and the fat and the strong I will watch over; I will feed them in justice. And I will set up over them one shepherd, my servant David, and he shall feed them (Ezek. 34:15-16,23).

He further promised:

> And will do more good to you than ever before. Then you will know that I am the Lord. From all your uncleannesses, and from all your idols I will cleanse you. A new heart I will give you, and a new spirit I will put within you (Ezek. 36:11,25-26).

Jeremiah spoke of the new covenant that God would establish with His people (31:31-34). While Ezekiel (37:25;28:25) and Jeremiah (30:10;46:27) spoke of Israel as God's servant, the servant poems in Isaiah are the clearest descriptions of Israel as God's redeeming servant for the world (42:1-4;49:1-6;50:4-9;52:13 to 53:12). It is not always clear of whom the prophet was speaking and scholars give varying interpretations. It is clear, however, that God intended through Israel to go on with His purpose of redemption.

Daniel spoke mysteriously of a heavenly Son of man as the one who would establish God's true kingdom (7:13-14.). At times the future revelation was described as the restoration of David's glorious kingdom, ruled over by a prince from the house of David (Mic. 5:2 *ff.*). Joel spoke about God pouring out His Spirit on all flesh (2:28-29).

The Old Testament has many references to the "Lord's anointed." Prophets, priests, and kings were anointed with oil as a sign that God had chosen them for their offices. It was to be expected, therefore, that the future King chosen by God would also be His "anointed One." The future king was never explicitly called "the Messiah" but would indeed bear all the characteristics of an "anointed one." Out of all the varied descriptions of the coming revelation and redemption, the one God appointed to bring it to pass could properly be called "the Messiah." In Jewish writings between the Old and New Testaments, the term *Messiah* began to appear as the title of the one whom God would raise up to restore David's kingdom and was applied to a human "son of David."[4]

Since God's future revelation would be accomplished by one especially anointed by Him, the term *Messiah* in time became a title for that future king. Whether the name actually appears, we can still properly speak of the "messianic hope" of the Old Testament, therefore, in all its varied forms.

From the perspective of the New Testament, which proclaims Jesus as the Messiah, many passages in the Old Testament referring to the "Lord's anointed" are seen to be fulfilled in Him.

The Old Testament looks to the future.—The revelation in the Old Testament arises out of the dynamic presence and movement of God in Israel's history. Due to mankind's sinful inclination to idolatry, it even took God time to make Himself known. Yet the revelation recorded there is not complete. We thus speak of the Old Testament as a preparatory revelation. It is full of promise of a still greater, plainer, and more dynamic self-disclosure of God as He moved forward with His purpose of redemption for all the world. That complete and supreme revelation is to be found in the New Testament. Now the two must be taken together if one is to have the full account of God's special revelation in history. Without the New Testament, the

Old Testament remains unfinished, incomplete, and unfulfilled. Without the Old Testament, the New Testament cannot be understood or fully appreciated as part of the total witness to God's mighty acts of revelation and redemption. Only the two together comprise the "Bible," properly speaking.

The Supreme Revelation

The Word Made Flesh

The central heartbeat of the biblical revelation is God's revelation of Himself. The revelation arises out of a divine/human encounter. God reveals Himself in all His works, so the revelation in the creation is part of the preparatory revelation. It is through persons that He makes Himself known. In the Old Testament, it was through inspired spokesmen that God interpreted His presence, His mighty acts, His providence, and His redeeming grace among His covenant people. What He has revealed there is that He is the only God, Creator, Judge and Redeemer, Lord of nature and history, perfect in His holiness, righteousness, mercy, grace, and love.

As the Creator of all things, God is the source of human life and all blessings. He has endowed us with the ability to respond to Him in loving obedience, to be colaborers with Him in the fulfillment of His purpose in creation. As the holy God, He opposes our sinfulness and idolatry, yet out of His grace, He seeks our redemption. All this we learn from the revelation in the Old Testament, which comes to full flower and fruition in the New Testament.

The deity of Jesus as the Christ.—The chief witness to Jesus in the New Testament has to do with God making Himself known through Jesus. The deity of Jesus is so entertwined with His humanity that the two cannot be separated. God Himself is met in Jesus. In Him the supreme revelation takes place. He fulfills the preparatory revelation of the Old Testament whose main features become embodied in Him.

God's revelation in the New Testament takes place in a historical event, in a particular person, in a datable time and place. All is now concentrated in the life, death, and resurrection of Jesus Christ.

In many and various ways God spoke of old to our fathers by the prophets; but in these last days he has spoken to us by a Son, whom he appointed heir of all things, through whom also he created the world. He reflects the glory of God and bears the very stamp of his nature, upholding the universe by his word of power (Heb. 1:1-3)

As in the Old Testament, God is His own interpreter. So He inspired John to write:

In the beginning was the Word, and the Word was with God, and the Word was God. He was in the beginning with God; all things were made through him, and without him was not anything made that was made. And the Word became flesh and dwelt among us, full of grace and truth; we have beheld his glory, glory as of the only Son from the Father. For the law was given through Moses; grace and truth came through Jesus Christ. No one has ever seen God; the only Son, who is in the bosom of the Father, he has made him known" (John 1:1-3,14,17-18).

In the Old Testament the Word of God and the prophet are two separate entities. In the New Testament, Jesus is the Living Word, through whom God reveals the true nature of His personal being. So John reported the word of Jesus, "He who has seen me has seen the Father" (John 14:9). God Himself makes Himself known in the life of Jesus. In Him is the supreme revelation of God's character, power, and purpose.

Paul bore the same witness when he wrote, "For God, who commanded the light to shine out of darkness, hath shined in our hearts, to give the light of the knowledge of the glory of God in the face of Jesus Christ" (2 Cor. 4:6, KJV). Reference to the "face" emphasizes the divine/human encounter as the essential form in which the revelation of God must take place. To confront Jesus is to meet God Himself incarnate in His humanity.

The New Testament witness to God's presence in Jesus makes plain that it is the God of creation, the God of the Old Testament, who is making Himself known. It means that the God who "in the beginning" (Gen. 1:1; John 1:1), created all things by the power of His Word (Heb. 1:3), by that same Word now speaks to us in Jesus' life. God's original purpose in creation is now made plain in Him.

The humanity of Jesus.—God made His most direct and personal contact with us in the humanity of Jesus. No truth is plainer in the New Testament than that Jesus was truly and fully human, just as He was truly and fully divine. The Gospels record clearly how very human He was: He hungered, He grew weary, He expressed anger, He wept, He was "tempted as we are, yet without sin" (Heb. 4:15).

We encounter the genuineness of Jesus' humanity in His temptations and sufferings. His struggle in the wilderness with the evil one was no mock battle, put on for mere show. And the struggle went on throughout His life, even in Gethsemane and up to the cross itself— "And when the devil had ended every temptation, he departed from him until an opportune time" (Luke 4:13).

As a man, Jesus drew His strength constantly through prayer.

> In the days of his flesh, Jesus offered up prayers and supplications, with loud cries and tears, to him who was able to save him from death, and he was heard for his godly fear. Although he was a Son, he learned obedience through what he suffered; and being made perfect he became the source of eternal salvation to all who obey him (Heb. 5:7-9).

God used Jesus' temptations, sufferings, prayers, and struggles to convince us that He identifies with our own humanity. "For we have not a high priest who is unable to sympathize with our weaknesses." Thus we can "with confidence draw near to the throne of grace, that we may receive mercy and find grace to help in time of need" (Heb. 4:15-16).

Jesus' humanity is further attested in Luke's infancy narrative, "And Jesus increased in wisdom and in stature, and in favor with God and man" (Luke 2:52). Here, as in Hebrews, we are told that Jesus, as a human being, had to grow into maturity. As the special "earthen vessel" through whom God made His supreme revelation of himself, it is not necessary to ascribe omniscience to Jesus, which He himself disclaimed in speaking of the eschaton (end time)—"But of that day or that hour no one knows, not even the angels in heaven, nor the Son, but only the Father" (Mark 13:32).

Aware of God's redemptive revelation in history, Paul testified to Jesus' true humanity throughout his epistles. "But when the time had fully come, God sent forth his Son, born of woman, born under the law, to redeem those who were under the law, so that we might receive adoption as sons" (Gal. 4:4-5.). Again he wrote, "For as by man came death, by a man has come also the resurrection of the dead" (1 Cor. 15:21). He further spoke of Jesus as God's unique Son "who was descended from David according to the flesh, and designated Son of

God in power according to the Spirit of holiness by his resurrection from the dead, Jesus Christ our Lord" (Rom. 1:3).

Jesus' human mortality is nowhere more plainly stated than in the descriptions of Him bleeding and dying on the cross, preceded by His human cry, "My God, my God, why hast thou forsaken me?" (Mark 15:34).

Throughout, the New Testament is consistent in its testimony as to the true humanity of Jesus. In many passages the stress is made as an effort to combat the rising heresy of Docetism which held that Jesus only "appeared" to be human. His miraculous conception in Mary is as much an affirmation of Jesus' humanity as His deity. Any doctrine of Christ which minimizes His humanity seriously distorts the clear witness of the New Testament.

As in the Old Testament, revelation is unto redemption. In the New Testament, that redemption is brought to fulfillment, reaching its climax in the death and resurrection of Jesus. His death is both the once-for-all sufficient sacrifice and atonement for the sins of the world and the sacrifice that establishes the new covenant as God promised in Jeremiah.

The revealing presence of God in historical event, the giving of His Word, the showing of His face, and the creation of a new covenant community of faith are now focused and completed in the presence of God in and through the life, death, and resurrection of Jesus. In Him is God's complete, final, and supreme revelation.

Christ the living Word.—All the promises of the preparatory revelation have their fulfillment in Jesus Christ. He fulfills the symbolism of the sacrificial system in His atoning death. His teachings fulfill the role of the prophets of old. As the Lord's anointed, He is the promised Messiah-King who reveals the true nature of God's lordship and kingdom. And He does so as God's living Word. His personhood and work are the embodiment of the divine revelation.

As Paul put it so graphically, "God was in Christ reconciling the world to himself. For in him the whole fulness of deity dwells bodily" (2 Cor. 5:19; Col. 2:9).

The Witness of the Apostles

The gospel proclaimed.—As God raised up the prophets in the Old Testament as His chosen interpreters, so in the New Testament the apostles fulfilled the essential role of interpreting God's revelation of Himself in Jesus. Since God's ultimate purpose was to reveal His redemption for all people everywhere the apostles were sent forth with the message of God's good news.

In doing so, they continued to interpret who Jesus is and what He has done for the redemption of the world. Beyond the life of Jesus Himself, God continues, through His Holy Spirit, to be present in and work through the new covenant community of faith, the church.

An essential element in the apostles' witness was to draw out the full implication of Jesus' humanity and deity and to show why faith affirms God's revealing and redeeming presence in Him. They did not speculate as philosophers. With the aid of the Holy Spirit, they testified out of their own experience that they had met God in Jesus Christ.

Without downgrading the true humanity of Jesus, Paul's chief stress was on the preexistent Son of God, who as the exalted Christ is now the living Redeemer, available through God's Spirit unto salvation to all who believe.

In a classic passage from Philippians Paul set forth the full sweep of God's revelatory redemption in Jesus Christ:

> Have this mind among yourselves, which is yours in Christ Jesus, who, though he was in the form of God, did not count equality with God a thing to be grasped, but emptied himself, taking the form of a servant, being born in the likeness of men. And being found in human form he humbled himself and became obedient unto death, even death on a cross. Therefore, God has highly exalted him and bestowed on him the name which is above every name, that at the name of Jesus every knee should bow, in heaven and on earth and under the earth, and every tongue confess that Jesus Christ is Lord, to the glory of God the Father (Phil. 2:5-11).

Much scholarly debate has revolved around the meaning of "emptied himself." For some it meant the eternal Son of God laid aside His divine attributes of omnipotence, omniscience, and omnipresence in order to become truly human, while retaining fully the holiness of God's moral character. There are other scholars who do not see the meaning of "emptied himself" this way. For them Jesus was both God and man at the same time. Whatever else the term may have meant, it cannot mean that Jesus became just a human being. The tension of the divine and the human must be maintained in the incarnation of Jesus Christ.

Jesus' humanity is seen in His obedience as God's servant, yielding even to the death of the cross as God's will. Such obedience and humility merits His right to bear the name Lord, God's own name of saving covenant love.

In late Judaism, out of a sense of sinfulness in the presence of God, the Jews substituted *adonai* ("Lord") when coming on the covenant name Yahweh as given to Moses. In the Septuagint (a Greek translation of the Hebrew Scriptures from the second century BC in Alexandria, supposedly by seventy scholars, hence the designation LXX), *adonai* was translated by *kurios,* "Lord."

To call Jesus "Lord" is to acknowledge God's unique presence in Him. It was Paul's favorite designation for Christ and is the fundamental confession of the New Testament (Rom. 10:9; John 20:13,28).

In Hebrews Jesus becomes God's "once-for-all" sacrifice for sin which does away with animal sacrifices. In Him God provided the all-sufficient atonement, making Him our eternal high priest.

Throughout the New Testament other terms are used to designate who Jesus is: *Logos* (God's eternal creating and saving power); Savior (Phil. 3:20); the Alpha and Omega (Rev. 1:17; see Isa. 44:6); the living one (Rev. 1:18, frequently of God in the Old Testament); the Lamb of God (John 1:29); Son of man (Jesus' own favorite designation of himself); Emmanuel (Matt. 1:23; see Isa. 7:14).

The messianic title *Messiah* ("Christ") became part of Jesus' personal name and is used throughout the New Testament. But the most important designation for Jesus is the "Son of God." The overwhelming testimony of the New Testament is that God has sent His only Son to be the Messiah. The Gospels reflect Jesus' consciousness of sonship as His own deepest awareness of who He is. Luke traces it back into His boyhood (Luke 2:49).

In His baptism, Jesus' consciousness of sonship is linked also with His awareness of being God's special Servant, combining quotations from a messianic psalm and a servant poem from Isaiah. "Thou art my beloved Son; with thee I am well pleased" (Luke 3:22; Ps. 2:7; Isa. 42:1). The temptations in the wilderness likewise report Jesus' struggle with the evil one over the meaning of His sonship. In time the apostolic witness could no longer make a distinction between the deity of Jesus and God Himself, while still affirming His true humanity. In Him God's Word had become flesh. The revelation of God had reached its fulfillment.

The message preserved.—In time the Gospels were written and the letters of Paul and the other New Testament writings became widely circulated. Already possessing the Old Testament Scriptures, the church of the new covenant had as its stewardship the full accounts of God's redeeming revelation in written form. But it was not until the fourth century AD that the church arrived at an acceptable canon of Holy Scriptures as the authentic record of God's special revelation of Himself in history. Henceforth the Bible became the written form of God's revelation.

The Indispensable Bible

We can know who God is because He has revealed Himself. This is the central claim of the Bible. In it God continues to speak to all who will listen with prayerful hearts and open minds. No other book can take its place. It arose out of the revealing events in which God has made Himself known. He is its central subject matter. It is aimed at our redemption. It seeks to draw us into our own divine/human encounter with God. It always points beyond itself to the living God, our Creator and Redeemer, known through personal faith in Jesus Christ as our Savior, whose death provided a perfect atonement for our sins.

By His resurrection, Christ is now available to us through God's own Holy Spirit, as Paul so aptly was inspired to remind us:

> If the Spirit of him who raised Jesus from the dead dwells in you, he who raised Christ Jesus from the dead will give life to your mortal bodies also through his Spirit that dwells in you (Rom. 8:11).

The doctrine of revelation is simply stated: God has made Himself known. The Bible is the record of His revelation. To know God as He has revealed Himself one must read the Bible and yield to its claims.

Opening its sacred pages, its truth becomes our own when we can sing with the poet as our own desire and confession:

> Break thou the bread of Life, Dear Lord to me,
> As thou didst break the loaves Beside the sea;

Beyond the sacred page I seek thee, Lord;
My spirit pants for thee, O living Word.[5]

Notes

1. Emil Brunner, *Revelation and Reason* (Philadelphia: The Westminster Press, 1946), p. 23.

2. Ibid.

3. Ibid., pp. 84-93.

4. Alan Richardson, Ed., *A Theological Word Book of the Bible* (New York: The Macmillan Company, 1951), p. 45.

5. The *Baptist Hymnal* (Nashville: Convention Press, 1975), "Break Thou the Bread of Life," Mary A. Lathbury, No. 138.

3
Revelation and Scripture

The Inspiration of the Biblical Writers

Revelation has to do with the times, places, and ways in which God has made Himself known to us (Heb. 1:1-4). An essential element in God's revealing acts was His use of inspired interpreters to proclaim, record, and preserve an authentic witness to His acts of revelation. Out of a vast array of literature, the selection of a special body of written records becomes an indispensable means whereby God continues to communicate Himself to us. The doctrine of inspiration affirms the faith that God Himself, through His Spirit, was directly involved in the writing, editing, collection, and preservation of this written witness to His revealing redemptive acts. The Bible became God's Word (His revealing and redemptive action in history) in written form.

Scripture as Witness to Revelation

The Primary Revelation.—Beyond its sacred pages, the Bible always points to the living God who has made Himself known. The revelation itself is prior to any written witness to it. It arises out of specific divine/human encounters with historical persons. It arises out of specific historical events. But neither the encounter nor the event is revelation until those involved were inspired by God to understand what God was saying and doing.

Interestingly enough not every encounter or event is of equal clarity as revelation. Nevertheless, each in its own way, is God saying something significant about Himself. The particular content and purpose in each event/encounter is related realistically to the need of the person, time, and place in which it occurs. God's person and purpose are more clearly seen and understood in some instances than in others. Moses' encounter with God, for example, is more revelatory of God's overall purpose than the account of Samson and Delilah, though the latter is part of God's continuing presence as Redeemer among His people.

The primary revelation, therefore, has to do with the event/encounters in which God has made Himself known. But we would not know of these revelatory acts of God had not an authentic interpretation of them been recorded and preserved.

The Record of God's Revelation.—The writings of the Old and New Testaments are the only authentic record that witness to God's special revelation in history. They are not the revelatory encounter/events themselves, but they are the inspired writings of those who experienced the encounters and witnessed the events. The Holy Scriptures also are authentic revelation because God continues to speak to us through them. They contain the true knowledge of the one and only true and living God. They contain, therefore, unique authority. We are able to hear the divine accent in every part again, God addressing us more clearly and directly in some parts than in others.

For example, we encounter the majestic holiness and saving grace of God more clearly in Isaiah, chapters 40—66, than in the genealogies of Genesis 11:10-32, though the latter is a necessary connecting link between God's saving, judging acts in the earlier accounts in Genesis leading up to his call of Abram. Romans, as a divine revelation of God's character and saving purpose, stands on a higher plain than Samuel and Kings, though both are equally inspired.

In fact, the whole New Testament stands on a higher plane than the entire Old Testament, for it witnesses to God's Word made flesh in Jesus Christ, the fulfillment of the preparatory revelation of the Old Testament. Taken together both record God's movement in history to make Himself known. One without the other cannot be properly understood.

As an analogy, we may liken the Bible to a jigsaw puzzle. Every part is essential if we are to get the whole picture, but the most important piece of the puzzle is the "facepiece" seen in Jesus Christ (John 14:9; 2 Cor. 4:6). He is God's final, supreme, authoritative revelation of

Himself. He remains the Living Word of revelation. "He reflects the glory of God and bears the very stamp of his nature" (Heb. 1:3*a*).

But we know this only through the witness of the New Testament. As witness to revelation, the Scripture is nonetheless revelation—but in written form. As God still speaks to us through its sacred pages, as witness to the true revelation of God, we quite properly call the Bible the Word of God.

Because it derives from the Holy God Himself we also speak of it as the Holy Bible. Yet it does not tell us everything possible to know about God. It concentrates on His revealing, saving acts in history. The created order is also His "book." (Ps. 19:1-2; Rom. 1:20). Science and even philosophy, under the guidance of Scripture, also reveal God, but not unto redemption. Such knowledge of God helps us to be the good stewards and servants of God as intended in creation.

The Bible itself reserves for the life and world to come our perfect knowledge of God—and that in a perfect divine/human encounter. "For now we see in a mirror dimly, but then face to face. Now I know in part; then I shall understand fully, even as I have been fully understood" (1 Cor. 13:12).

The Bible does not answer all the questions we could possibly ask about God, but it does answer the most important questions of life: how the Creator God who made us has acted in Jesus, out of His infinite grace and mercy, to redeem us; how God gives us His own Holy Spirit as wisdom and power to become at last what God intended for us to be; how He has provided for us a spiritual family in the church wherein we grow to spiritual maturity; how He has provided the Holy Scriptures as His continuing communion and communication with us.

The Biblical Claim to Inspiration

The Bible is God's indispensible, irreplaceable witness to His saving deeds on our behalf. Because it arose out of the historical acts of revelation, it is one of the revealing acts of God Himself. Believing faith affirms that God had a hand directly in the Bible's composition and preservation. The inspiration of those who wrote the Bible is a clear claim the Scriptures make for themselves.

The classical passages.—There are two main passages in the New Testament that speak directly about the inspiration of the Scriptures.

The longer and most extensive passage is found in Paul's admonition to Timothy.

> But as for you, continue in what you have learned and have firmly believed, knowing from whom you learned it and how from childhood you have been acquainted with the sacred writings which are able to instruct you for salvation through faith in Jesus Christ. All scripture is inspired by God and profitable for teaching, for reproof, for correction, and for training in righteousness, that the man of God may be complete, equipped for every good work (2 Tim. 3:14-17).

The passage quite obviously refers to the Jewish Scriptures. Though known by Timothy from childhood, they were now interpreted from the perspective of "salvation through faith in Jesus Christ." Here is reflected the value, use, and purpose of the Old Testament Scriptures as understood by the early church.

Their authority as God's Word is attributed to their inspiration. Found nowhere else in the Bible, the word *theopneustos* literally means "God breathed," though examples may be found in pagan Greek literature.[1] It is a clear reference to God's Spirit as the ultimate source and energizing, directing power by which the sacred writings have come into existence.

No theory of inspiration is to be found here. Nothing is said about *how* the inspiration took place. Emphasis is laid on the purpose and result of God's inspiring activity. Able to lead us to a saving experience by faith in Jesus Christ, Scripture then guides us to spiritual maturity.

The second classical passage is found in 2 Peter 1:20-21.

> First of all you must understand this, that no prophecy of scripture is a matter of one's own interpretation, because no prophecy ever came by the impulse of man, but men moved by the Holy Spirit spoke from God.

Again reference is to the Old Testament as it witnessed to Jesus Christ (2 Peter 1:16-17). No explanation as to the mechanics of inspiration is made. The author reflected the prevailing conviction in Judaism that Scripture derives from the divine activity through men under the influence of God's Spirit.

The Bible does not spell out any theory on how inspiration took place. It was not until the Reformation, when the authority of Scripture was set over against the traditions of the Roman Church, that serious attention was given to the manner of inspiration.[2] There has never been a universally agreed upon definition of inspiration accepted by all Christians. Later theories sought to clarify how the concept of inspiration was to be related to how active or passive the recipient was, the meaning of revelation, the actual words of the Bible itself, the nature of biblical authority, and the biblically stated purpose of Scripture.

Other biblical passages.—Inspiration means that God was directly involved in the writing of Scripture. The claim is clearly affirmed in many other passages although the term *inspiration* does not appear. "Thus saith the Lord" is a recurrent phrase in the Old Testament. The prophets universally testified that their words came from God. Various apostles made the same claim for the message they proclaimed. As for example: "Aaron spoke all the words which the Lord had spoken to Moses" (Ex. 4:30). "The Lord said to Moses, Now therefore write this song, and teach it to the people of Israel; put it in their mouths, that this song may be a witness for me. So Moses wrote this song the same day, and taught it to the people of Israel" (Deut. 31:14,19,22). "Now these are the last words of David. The Spirit of the Lord speaks by me, his word is upon my tongue, the God of Israel has spoken, the Rock of Israel has said to me" (2 Sam. 23:1a-3). "Then the Lord put forth his hand and touched my mouth; and the Lord said to me, 'Behold, I have put my words in your mouth' " (Jer. 1:9).

"This word came to Jeremiah from the Lord; take a scroll and write on it all the words that I have spoken to you against Israel and Judah and all the nations, from the day I spoke to you, from the days of Josiah until today" (Jer. 36:1b-2). Jeremiah, Ezekiel, Hosea, Joel, Amos, Obadiah, Jonah, Micah, Nahum, Habakkuk, Zephaniah, Haggai, Zechariah, and Malachi all make the specific claim that "the word of the Lord came" to them.

Following in the train of the great prophets, Jesus declared, "For I have not spoken on my own authority; the Father who sent me has himself given me commandment what to say and what to speak" (John 12:49). The author of Hebrews attributed the Old Testament to God's Holy Spirit (Heb. 3:7; 4:7). Paul claimed his words also came from God, "And we impart this in words not taught by human wisdom but taught by the Spirit, interpreting spiritual truths to those who possess the Spirit" (1 Cor. 2:13).

On a par with the claim of the ancient prophets, Paul testified that his message came from beyond himself.

> For I would have you know, brethren, that the gospel which was preached by me is not man's gospel. For I did not receive it from man, nor was I taught it, but it came through a revelation of Jesus Christ (Gal. 1:11-12). If any one thinks that he is a prophet, or spiritual, he should acknowledge that what I am writing to you is a command from the Lord (1 Cor. 14:37).

Second Peter also elevates the writings of Paul to a stature equal to the Old Testament writings.

> So also our beloved brother Paul wrote to you according to the wisdom given him, speaking of this as he does in all his letters. There are some things in them hard to understand, which the ignorant and unstable twist to their own destruction, as they do the other scriptures (2 Pet. 3:15-16).

In time, therefore, inspiration was attributed to all of the New Testament and thus to the entire Bible as God's written Word.

Theories of Inspiration

With the rise of modern science following the Reformation, new challenges to biblical authority became apparent. The Enlightenment intensified the challenge by emphasizing the autonomy of human reason, the development of the fields of comparative religions and the psychology of religion, and the new scientific methods of biblical research. The effort to define more precisely the meaning of inspiration became, therefore, a recurring issue in Christian theology. The basic questions were: How can we relate the human and the divine elements so apparent in Scripture? how can we define the trustworthiness of Scripture as God's authoritative Word for saving faith? how can we relate inspiration and revelation? and how can we come to terms with the truths of modern science without doing violence to the abiding truth of scriptural claims? Over the years a number of theories of inspiration have been proposed. A summary and critique of several theories follows.

General intuition.[3]—This view holds that the inspiration of the biblical writers was no different in kind than the elevated natural insight and intelligence found among the great philosophers, artists, and musicians. To be sure the genius of Shakespeare, Plato, Milton, Handel, Beethoven, and others of like stature, exhibit a heightened expression of mankind's superior intellect as created by God in His image.

To assume the biblical writers wrote only out of general intuition is to invalidate the biblical claim that they wrote as "moved by the Holy Spirit." It assumes "that natural insight is the only source of religious truth" and regards the Bible "as the product of man's own powers."[4]

This view is inadequate to describe the uniqueness of biblical inspiration. It obscures the biblical claim to revelation as God taking the initiative to make Himself known in historical events.

General illumination.—This view is really a refinement of the intuition theory. It stresses the inspiration of the writers whose thoughts were inspired by God but who were left on their own in the choice of their words. It does call attention to the cooperative effort of God and man so evident in the Bible.

In distinction from the original inspiration, many scholars use the term *illumination* to designate the aid of the Holy Spirit in helping one to understand the revelation of God in Scripture. At times, however, illumination is one form of inspiration as when God enables someone in the New Testament better to understand what he already knew, namely when quoting from the Old Testament.

Mechanical dictation.—This view assumes the total passivity of the biblical writer. He acted only as a penman, as though God dictated His revelation into a tape recorder. Its chief emphasis is on the actual words of the Bible. Athenagoras, a second-century apologist, "held that the Spirit lifted the prophets into ecstasy, breathing into them as a flute-player breathes into a flute."[5] However, this was not the view generally held by the early church fathers.

In the Council of Trent, the Roman Church challenged the Protestant principle of *sola scriptura* (Scripture alone as the authoritative source of divinely revealed truth). Afterward Protestant leaders were driven more and more to assert the Bible as the "very words of God" and to conceive of revelation as the giving of certain theological propositions about God.

Extreme conclusions were often drawn from this position. "The Swiss Formula of Consensus of 1675 not only called the Scriptures 'the very word of God,' but declared the Hebrew vowel-points to be inspired, and some theologians traced them back to Adam."[6]

The dictation theory does less than justice to a proper understanding of biblical inspiration. It produces a Docetic view of the Bible by denying that God worked in and through human beings. (Docetism was an early church heresy that held that Jesus only "appeared" to be human.) The Docetic view often leads to a crass literalism in interpretation that ignores the true humanity of the Bible and provides an inadequate basis for coming to terms with the truths of modern science.

Today not even the most conservative scholars hold to the dictation theory of inspiration. It provides no basis for understanding the Bible both as a divine and a human production.

The verbal/plenary theory.—This view holds that the words of the Bible are an essential part of the divine revelation and that the Bible is inspired in all its parts. Plenary (in full) is taken in two senses. It means every book is equally inspired; the whole Bible is the result of divine inspiration.

In a more specialized sense, it means that inspiration applies to every kind of knowledge encountered in the Scriptures. While disclaiming the Bible as "a textbook on chemistry, astronomy, philosophy, or medicine," nevertheless "when it speaks on matters having to do with these or any other subjects, the Bible does not lie to us."[7] The Bible is viewed as being free from errors of all kinds.

One obvious strength of this view is that it takes seriously the divine element in the Scriptures. It emphasizes that since the Bible communicates through words, the words (not just the ideas) must be inspired. This view differs from the human dictation theory by seeking to balance the inspiration of the Spirit with the human capacities of each writer. The weakness in this view is the tendency to so emphasize the propositional truth of the Bible that the personal nature of faith is subordinated to belief in propositions (statements of the Bible).

The dynamic theory.—While holding to a clear view of the inspiration of Scripture, this view understands inspiration more as "a matter of the message of God's salvation than the method or process by which it was reduced to written form. The authority of the Bible is in its wholeness and unity in the light of the truth of God in Christ."[8]

The emphasis is more on the function of Scripture than an effort to fully explain the process of inspiration. It seeks to take the humanity of the Bible as seriously as it takes the divine element so apparent in Scripture. It seeks to stress the dynamic nature of revelation that arises out of the actual realities of human history. It takes seriously the unfolding, progressive response to God's accumulative revelation as it finally reached its fullness in the Word made flesh in Jesus Christ. The weakness in this view is the tendency to overstress the human element in Scripture and to depend too much on human wisdom to judge the truthfulness of its divine message.

The Evidences of Inspiration

No single theory of inspiration has universal acceptance. There are strengths and weaknesses in all theories. Competent scholars can be found to hold one view or the other. The final authority of the Bible does not rest on any particular theory. The claim to be inspired is not the major claim the Bible makes for itself. Its major claim is that it is able to make us "wise unto salvation that is in Jesus Christ."

Perhaps no better definition of inspiration can be found than that expressed by A. H. Strong:

> Inspiration is that influence of the Spirit of God upon the minds of the Scripture writers which made their writings the record of a progressive divine revelation, sufficient, when taken together and interpreted by the same Spirit who inspired them, to lead every honest inquirer to Christ and to salvation.[9]

The biblical witness to itself.—The Bible witnesses to its own inspiration in three major ways: the claim of the prophets and apostles that God spoke through them; the direct ascription of inspiration to its writings (2 Tim. 3:14-17; 2 Peter 1:20-21); and the unity of the Bible running through its sixty-six books.

The urgency with which the prophets spoke and their inability to resist God's claim upon them (Isa. 6; "If I say, 'I will not mention him,/or speak any more in his name,'/there is in my heart as it were a burning fire/shut up in my bones,/and I am weary with holding it in,/and I cannot" Jer. 20:9; "And the Lord took me from following the flock, and the Lord said to me, 'Go, prophesy to my people Israel' " Amos 7:15) testify to the prophets' true encounters with God.

Paul expressed the same constraint, "Woe to me if I do not preach the gospel! . . . I am entrusted with a commission" (1 Cor. 9:16-17).

Such urgency is felt throughout Scripture. The overwhelming witness is that God is present, leading, judging, redeeming, and speaking in the life and experience of the biblical writers.

Even when the word *inspiration* is not used, one is aware of its reality. Such phrases as "thus saith the Lord," "the word of the Lord came," and "thus it is written" occur throughout the Bible's pages.

No single writer of any portion of the Bible was aware of the whole Bible as we now have it. Each one spoke and wrote out of the peculiar realities of his own historical situation, to the need of his special hearers. The divine revelation was conveyed through many literary forms and in various ways (Heb. 1:1). God's Word was expressed through the vocabulary and cultural thought forms familiar to those being addressed. But in the midst of all this variety, one is aware that it is the same God making himself known. The unity of the Bible is discerned in the coherence of the unfolding revelation as arising from the same source. The written Word of God always points beyond its sacred pages to the same living God who is the singular Author of the divine disclosure.

Inspiration confirmed in the experience of faith.—The Bible declares its own purpose of inspiration: The sacred writings are able to instruct us in salvation through faith in Jesus Christ, for "All [every] scripture is inspired by God and profitable for teaching, for reproof, for correction, and for training in righteousness, that the man of God may be complete, equipped for every good work" (2 Tim. 3:16-17).

The Scriptures invite us to test the spirits (1 John 4:1), to put its claims to the test of believing faith. It promises the Spirit who inspired Scripture as our teacher. "But the Counselor, the Holy Spirit, whom the Father will send in my name, he will teach you all things, and bring to remembrance all that I have said to you" (John 14:26).

While the Bible contains objective truth about God, it is not known as such without the aid of "the inner testimony of the Spirit," as the Reformers constantly stressed. Through His written Word, God continues to speak to all who will listen unto the end that the living Word, Jesus Christ, may Himself address us.

The continuation of inspiration.—Some writers use "illumine" to describe what the Spirit does to help us respond to inspired Scripture. The Christian life is to be a Spirit-filled life. Through His Spirit the risen Christ now dwells in our hearts by faith (Rom. 8:9-16; 2 Cor. 4:6; Col. 1:27).

The purpose of this continuing inspiration is not to give any new revelation that carries us beyond what God has already said in Jesus Christ. It is rather to make Him known. "When the Spirit of truth comes, He will glorify me, for he will take what is mine and declare it to you" (John 16:13,14).

As the Spirit was the author of Scripture, so He is promised to be the interpreter of Scripture. He fulfills the purpose of Scripture by instructing us out of its sacred pages. As the revelation of God arose out of a divine/human encounter, the record of which is found in the Bible, so now God uses Scripture to draw us into our own saving encounter with Him.

The Bible was not dropped down entire from heaven as a single volume. It did not come into existence all at once. It is a collection of many books written over a period of about fifteen hundred years. It exhibits a rich variety of literary forms, all of which reflect the human cultural situation of each writer. It is the Word of God in the words of men, God accommodating Himself to the vocabulary and thought forms of those He inspired to interpret His revealing, saving presence.

Unlike the Koran, believed to be an exact duplicate of a perfect book in heaven, handed down to a single prophet, Muhammad, the Bible arose out of the warp and woof of the tapestry of history which God was weaving over the years as a revelation of His purpose for us. It arose out of the agony and ecstasy of everyday life in the covenants God established with His chosen, first in Israel and completed in the final covenant ratified through the atoning death of Christ.

The doctrine of inspiration was arrived at out of the internal evidences of Scripture's witness to itself. It focuses not on the process of inspiration but on the purpose of Scripture to provide an authentic record of God's revealing and saving disclosure of Himself.

The Bible is not a book on science, general history, or even religion as such. It is a book about God. He is the main subject throughout its pages. It reaches its climax in the Incarnation, when the eternal *Logos* (God's creating and revealing power) is made flesh in Jesus Christ (John 1:14). All of God's revealing, redeeming activity in history becomes embodied in Him (Col. 2:9). Christ is the living Word, through whom, by His Spirit, God continues to address us in the agony and ecstasy of our everyday life. "For it is God who said, 'Let light shine out of darkness,' who has shone in our hearts to give the light of the knowledge of the glory of God in the face of Christ" (2 Cor. 4:6).

A Treasure in Earthen Vessels

Paul helped us understand something of the mystery of the nature and authority of Scripture as God's Word when he said: "But we have this treasure in earthen vessels, to show the transcendent power belongs to God and not to us" (2 Cor. 4:7).

The treasure of which Paul spoke is "the light of the knowledge of the glory of God in the face of Christ" (v. 6). That Paul had in mind himself as one of the "earthen vessels" is clear from the context. Despite his afflictions, perplexities, persecutions, and bearing the scars of faithfulness to Christ, God had used Paul mightily to proclaim salvation in Jesus' name. That Paul had endured these hardships and that many had believed through his preaching the gospel is evidence of God's transcendent power over all Paul's weaknesses and difficulties.

When Paul referred to vessels in the plural it indicates that he had more than himself in mind as one of God's earthen vessels. It refers as well to the words he used in preaching the gospel. Identifying himself with the Old Testament writers, Paul said, "Since we have the same spirit of faith as he had who wrote, 'I believed, and so I spoke,' we too believe, and so we speak" (v. 13, quoting Ps. 116:10).

By affirming his dependence upon the Old Testament Scriptures as divine guides for understanding Christ (v. 2), Paul seems to have included those Scriptures as one of the earthen vessels. If Paul considered himself an earthen vessel who knew the full revelation of God in Jesus Christ, no less must we consider as earthen vessels the writers of the preparatory revelation in the Old Testament.

Paul's inspired insight on the manner of God's workings provides a graphic metaphor for understanding the human element in Scripture. But we must not miss Paul's major emphasis—God's use of earthen vessels is "to show that the transcendent power belongs to God and not to us."

The most sublime expression of the metaphor applies to the incarnation of God's Word made flesh in Jesus Christ. He, too, is an earthen vessel in whose perfect humanity God most clearly displayed His transcendent power and glory.

Throughout Christian history many theologians have used the incarnation of Christ as a fit analogy for understanding the divine/human nature of Scripture. Clement, Origen, and Chrysostom used it, as did Calvin. Luther spoke of "the vessel of Christ's incarnate body." He further stated, "In order to grasp the biblical revelation in its fullness it is necessary to conceive of Scripture in terms of the divine-human nature of Christ."[10]

Types of Literature in the Bible

One of the indications that the Bible is an earthen vessel is seen in its great variety of literary forms. This is clear evidence that "in many and various ways God spoke of old to our fathers by the prophets" (Heb. 1:1), as He did also in the New Testament.

The Septuagint translation rearranged the order of the Hebrew Old Testament and roughly grouped the writings according to the types of literature they exhibited and has carried through to our present English copies. One must observe, however, that many books display more than one strand of literary form.

Law and instruction.—The opening books of the Bible are called the Pentateuch, or the Torah (Law): Genesis, Exodus, Leviticus, Numbers, and Deuteronomy. However, the giving of God's laws to His people is set in a historical narrative, climaxing in the Exodus deliverance and the establishing of the covenant at Sinai, and the movement of God's people toward the Promised Land.

The laws include instruction on morals, social customs, priestly requirements, proper sacrifices, and religious commandments as the Ten Commandments were applied to the total life of God's people.

Subsequent books of the Old Testament continue this instruction as well. The New Testament also contains a great deal of moral and religious instruction in the light of the life and teachings of Christ.

Historical narrative.—The specific books of history of the Old Testament include Joshua, Judges, Samuel, and Kings (called the Former Prophets because they bear the imprint of prophetic interpretation), Ruth, Ezra, Nehemiah, and Esther. These books relate Israel's special history as the sphere in which the divine revelation took place.

In the New Testament, the four Gospels and Acts recount the climactic event of historical revelation in Jesus Christ and the movement of Christianity out into the world.

Poetry and figures of speech.—Also known as Wisdom Literature, the poetic books of the Old Testament are Job, Psalms, Proverbs, Ecclesiastes, and the Song of Solomon. But most of the prophetic writings are cast in poetic form as well, while poems and songs can be found in some of the historical books.

As a way of thinking and speaking, figures of speech abound throughout the biblical literature, including the New Testament. The apostles often quote from early Christian hymns. Such passages warn us against a literal interpretation, while making God's revelation come alive with their vivid imagery.

Prophetic writings.—The person and function of the prophet in Israel was unique in the history of the ancient Near East. The earlier prophets were little more than soothsayers. But in Israel the role took on a far more serious function: They became the inspired interpreters of God's judging/redeeming presence and purpose among His people. In the Former Prophets (Joshua, Judges, Samuel, and Kings), six prophets were named but their oracles have not been preserved: Samuel, Nathan, Gad, Micaiah, Elijah, and Elisha.

The great age of prophecy began with Samuel and reached its classical expression in the Latter Prophets, grouped as the Major Prophets—Isaiah, Jeremiah, Lamentations, Ezekiel, and Daniel (though Daniel is listed among the Writings in the Hebrew text)—and the Twelve Minor Prophets in one scroll.

The prophets are best understood when seen against the background of four major historical crises in Israel, again helping us to understand revelation arising out of historical events: Amos, Hosea, Isaiah 1—39, and Micah against the decline and fall of Samaria in the Assyrian period; Zephaniah, Nahum, Habakkuk, and Jeremiah against the decline and fall of Judah in the Assyrian-Babylonian period; Ezekiel and Isaiah 40—66 in the Exile in the Babylonian period; and Haggai, Zechariah, Malachi, Obadiah, Joel, Jonah (Daniel, Chronicles, Ezra-Nehemiah also belong here historically) against the restoration in the Persian period.[11]

The prophetic books exhibit a rich variety of form: songs, poems, figures of speech, history, diatribes, autobiography, and moral and religious instruction. Called to pronounce God's judgments, they were often lonely and somber figures. But they also promised God's deliverance. They were first forthtellers of God's will and purpose in a given situation. They were often God's foretellers as they proclaimed God's promise for the future.

Israel's literature reached its high-water mark in the prophets in the unfolding of the preparatory revelation that moved toward its fulfillment in Jesus Christ, the promised Messiah.

No single book of the New Testament matches exactly the prophetic books of the Old Testament. Yet the New Testament throughout reflects the mind, spirit, and insight of the biblical prophet.

Apocalyptic writings.—Written mainly in symbolic code imagery, apocalyptic writings were "tracts for hard times." They arose in times of persecution to give encouragement to God's distressed people. Unveiling the secret things of God's future plans, they provided reassuring hope for troubled Israel. Daniel and the Book of Revelation (The Apocalypse) are the chief examples in the Bible. Shorter apocalyptic passages are found in Ezekiel, Isaiah, and Mark.

Gospels.—The books recording the life, death, and resurrection of Jesus are in a class by themselves. They are not strict biography in the modern sense of the word. There was nothing like it in the ancient world until adoring faith with inspired insight interpreted the meaning of Jesus' life as God's final and complete revelation of Himself in history. The term *gospel* ("good news") was first used to describe the message proclaimed by the apostles of God's saving action in Jesus. Because He was the message, the Word made flesh, it came in time to describe the written account of His life as well.

It is important to distinguish between the Synoptic Gospels (Matthew, Mark, and Luke) and John's Gospel. The literary style is quite different, but all tell the same story of Jesus' life and agree in their interpretation of Him as God's unique Son, the Messiah. All four stress the historical reality of Christ.

Epistles and sermons.—The letters of the apostles constitute the bulk of the New Testament writings. They were written to meet specific needs of the churches. Certain ones are more theological in purpose than others (Romans, Galatians, Colossians, Hebrews, for example). They are extremely personal in tone. Some were addressed to specific churches, others to the Christian community at large, a few to individual persons. Each reflects the gospel as preached and understood by the writer. All testify to God's saving action in Jesus Christ.

A few sermons are to be found in various parts of the Bible, as in some of the prophetic books and in the early chapters of Acts. Fragments of early Christian hymns and baptismal confessions are discernible in the letters of Paul.

Parables.—Special attention should be called to the parable, so distinctive in the teaching of Jesus. He did not invent the form but used it as His main method of teaching. "With many such parables he spoke the word to them, as they were able to hear it; he did not speak to them without a parable" (Mark 4:33-34).

The settings of Jesus' matchless stories were lifted out of the everyday experiences of His hearers. They were mirrors held up to life itself. Through their vivid imagery and aliveness, God spoke His word of redeeming grace to all "who had ears to hear." More than mere "earthly stories with a heavenly meaning," they were revelatory of God's kingdom, grace, and character.

As did the ancient prophets, Jesus also used the "enacted parable" on many occasions. Among such were the cleansing of the Temple, riding into Jerusalem on a donkey, washing the disciples' feet, the feeding of the multitude, and, supremely, the cross where deed and word were perfectly united as God's mighty act of redemption. Indeed, we might say that the whole life, death, and resurrection of Jesus was God's enacted parable of Himself in history.

Seen in its historical setting and in its own style and literary form, each book of the Bible fulfills its unique function as an earthen vessel through which God makes Himself known. Each contributes its own distinctive witness to the whole.

The Humanity of the Bible

Fallible men as true witnesses.—The principle of accommodation so widely used by the early church fathers and Reformers enabled them to come to terms with the humanity of the Bible. It protected them from crass literalism and the excesses of mystical interpretations to which many were prone. It allowed them to make important distinctions between the message of salvation and the form of the words in which it was couched.

The church fathers and Reformers constantly praised God that He could use weak and sinful human beings to accomplish His purposes. It enabled them to hold in harmony the divine and the human elements of Scripture. It helped them to understand God's use of anthropomorphisms as vehicles of revelation.

Several early Christian preachers and theologians spoke concerning God's use of human beings to write the Scriptures. Origen (AD 185?-?254) used the biblical figures of teacher and father to describe how God could communicate with us who are but as children in His sight. According to Chrysostom (AD 345?-407), God uses human ways of thinking and speaking, even "lisping" when He talks to us. Augustine (AD 354-430) used similar figures of speech to show God's condescension to our human limitations. All applied the principle of Christ's incarnation to the divine-human nature of Scripture.

Both Luther and Calvin applied the same principle of accommodation to the interpretation of Scripture. Their chief concern was to show that human limitations in speech and understanding in no way hindered the message of salvation getting through. Fallible men were accepted as true witnesses to the revelation entrusted to them, through whom the transcendent power of God was manifested.

Other evidences of the true humanity of the biblical writers are quite apparent. Inspiration does not mean God overrode the freedom and individuality of those through whom He spoke. The varied and individual style of the writer is clearly evident.

Each was a "child of his time" and culturally conditioned by the mores and customs prevalent in his particular situation. His speech and vocabulary reflected the common language of his peers.

The limited prescientific world knowledge of the biblical world must not be judged by our modern standards of accuracy, either in the fields of historical or scientific research. To claim that it is not the intention of Scripture to teach science but that the so-called prescientific view of the biblical world is part of the truth of revelation is to ignore the true humanity of the Bible and the Spirit's accommodation to the thought world of those He inspired with the message of God's redeeming revelation.

Augustine was insistent that the Scriptures do not teach science. In the controversy over Copernicus's new view of the solar system, Galileo is reported to have said, "The bible does not teach us how the stars go, but how to go to heaven." Yet the truthfulness of the Bible is seen in how it honestly reports how the phenomena of nature appeared to ancient man. God spoke to the people in terms they could understand in order to get across His message of saving grace.

The divine unity of the Bible.—In no way does the humanity of the Scripture, as an earthen vessel, make the Bible any less capable of being a vehicle of divine revelation. Its very humanity enhances our awareness of the transcendent power of God that is present in it. That which gives the Bible its essential unity is the divine presence and power that courses through its sacred pages.

Believing and obedient faith affirm the conviction that by inspiration God and persons have been joined in a mutual activity whereby Scripture is both God's Word and man's word. How this can be remains a mystery to us, as does the incarnation. That it has actually happened, Scripture is its own best witness.

That is why the church fathers and the Reformers stressed "the inner witness of the Holy Spirit" as the One who confirms the authority of Scripture. That is why they put their main emphasis on the function of Scripture to "make us wise unto salvation" rather than on trying to unravel the mystery of the mechanics of inspiration.

The Infallibility of Scripture

Revelation as progressive response.—That the revelation of God took place over a long span of years is self-evident. If it had been merely a matter of dictating a book, He could have done that all at once in the beginning. We have to deal with it in the way it actually happened. Long years of preparation were necessary to lay the groundwork for the incarnation. Having made us with freedom, which He never violates, God must woo and win back our loving obedience freely chosen. The nature of sin and its dire consequences must be made plain that our need of redemption may be made plain. God must first reveal Himself as Lord of nature and history, who alone is God, Judge, and Redeemer. God's people must be prepared to receive the promise of a coming Redeemer.

Among a chosen people with whom he established a covenant of hope and promise, the unfolding revelation revealed a varied response. Through the years, there was an accumulative buildup of the revelation, making God's presence and power ever clearer to those chosen to receive it. Part of the revelatory purpose of God was to inspire interpreters to record and preserve a written record of God's mighty acts as an abiding and authentic witness to oncoming generations.

In the fullness of time, the promise was kept. In the incarnation, God's Word was made flesh. The work of redemption is complete. A new covenant is established. God's grace, love, mercy, and salvation are offered to all the world. Through the risen Lord Christ, God moves on through history to complete His purpose in creation.

Again He raised up inspired interpreters to record and preserve a written witness to His coming in Jesus Christ in which He fulfilled and completed the preparatory revelation already recorded. In time the Old and New Testaments were combined into one book, giving us the complete account of God's redeeming revelation of Himself in history. Its main concern is to make God and the way of salvation known to us. To that end it is completely reliable, infallible, and trustworthy.

Christ the clue to Scripture.—The central figure of the Bible is Jesus Christ. He is the fulfillment of the preparatory revelation. As the Word made flesh, through His teachings, miracles, and deeds, God speaks His final and complete Word, fulfilling all He said previously in the prophets of old. Through the atoning death of Jesus, God established a new covenant of grace, fulfilling all the symbolism of the ancient priesthood. Through the presence and power of God's kingdom in Jesus, God makes known the true nature of His sovereignty, fulfilling the symbolism of Israel's ancient kings, God's vice-regents among His people.

As Prophet, Priest, and King, as Redeemer and Savior, as God's Suffering Servant, Jesus is entitled to bear God's own name—the covenant name Lord by which He redeemed Israel from Egypt, watched over the nation through its long agonizing history, and prepared His people for the incarnation, and the resurrection.

As the risen Lord, by His Spirit, God the Creator, who is love, offers us salvation and life eternal. All this we know through Jesus Christ. He is the clue to Scripture. He is the infallible Way, the Truth, the Life.

Notes

1. *Faith and Mission,* Southeastern Baptist Theological Seminary, Volume 1, Spring 1984, "Scripture and Inspiration," Donald E. Cook, p. 58.

2. Dewey M. Beegle, *Scripture, Tradition, and Infallibility* (Grand Rapids: Eerdman's Publishing Company, 1973). "Prior to the period of the Reformation, no doctrinal statement on inspiration was ever formulated at the great councils convened by the church. Among the earliest creedal statements was the Belgic Confession of Faith (1561)." p. 141.

3. The following section draws heavily on: Augustus Hopkins Strong, *Systematic Theology* (Philadelphia: The Judson Press, 1907), pp. 202-222; and *Review and Expositor,* The Southern Baptist Theological Seminary, Spring 1974, "Biblical Inspiration and Interpretation," pp. 179-195.

4. Strong, pp. 202-203.

5. *Review and Expositor,* p. 179.

6. Strong, p. 209.

7. Harold Lindsell, *The Battle for the Bible* (Grand Rapids: Zondervan Publishing House, 1976), p. 18.

8. *The Broadman Bible Commentary,* Clifton J. Allen, gen. Ed. (Nashville: Broadman Press, 1969), p. 6.

9. Strong, p. 196.

10. Jack B. Rogers and Donald K. McKim, *The Authority and Interpretation of the Bible* (San Francisco: Harper and Row, 1979), p. 78.

11. James King West, *Introduction to the Old Testament* (New York: The Macmillan Co., 1971), p. 218.

4
The Preservation of the Written Witness

The Idea of a Canon

In the course of Israel's history, an extensive body of literature was produced. Out of all that was written, how did it happen that our present thirty-nine books were selected as the authoritative account of God's redeeming presence in Israel? As the apostles went forth to preach the gospel, in the course of the years, an extensive body of Christian literature also arose in the church. Why did it take the Christian community of faith over three hundred years to select our present twenty-seven books of the New Testament as the authoritative account of how God had fulfilled the preparatory revelation in Jesus Christ?

A General Definition of Canon

The term *canon* ("rule, measurement, yardstick") is the technical term used to designate the sixty-six books of the Bible as God's written Word. It is claimed that these books alone are the all-sufficient authoritative record of the divine revelation in Israel and the church.

First use of the term.—Originally the word *canon* ("reed") meant the rule used by carpenters and builders. By the middle of the second century (about AD 150), it was used to designate brief confessions of faith, as in baptism, and so the teaching recognized by the church as "that norm according to which all one's teachings and life must be conformed, as it comes from divine sources."[1] The process was underway for drawing up rules of faith and practice.

Its later application.—The first application of the term *canon* to the books of the New Testament was made by Athanasius in AD 367. His intent was simply to list those books acceptable to be read in public worship in contrast to those books designated as *apokrypha* ("suitable to be read in secret, that is, in private devotions"). Long before, the terms *testament* ("covenant") and *Holy Scripture* had been used to designate the books of the Old and New Testaments as possessing superior authority as the most authentic witness to God's revelation in Israel and the church. In time, the term *canon* became the technical term setting apart the biblical books as possessing this unique authority. The process was long and complex, and we have no document from those ancient times describing in detail how it took place.

The Stream of Biblical History

How the literature grew.—Many books of the Bible reveal by internal evidence that they contain materials drawn from many sources. The Old Testament writers refer to some twenty-four books from which they often quote.[2] Many references are made to the "book of Jasher [the Upright]" from which David's lament over Saul and Jonathan was drawn (2 Sam. 1:18) and the account in Joshua 10:13 of the sun standing still. Frequent quotations are taken from the "Book of the Wars of the Lord" (Num. 21:14). The writers of Kings and Chronicles make frequent reference to the "Chronicles of the Kings of Israel and Judah." Victory songs, dirges, and poems are cited from other works as well.

Many scholars believe several strands of material, now joined in a single narrative, can be discerned in the early books of the Bible. Each is marked by its own peculiar style, vocabulary, theme, and purpose. Along with other minor strands, all serve as tributaries flowing into the mighty stream of Israel's history, whose chief emphasis was to recount God's providential choice of Israel as His chosen instrument of special revelation.

Not all scholars believe that the Pentateuch is made up of several sources now blended into one narrative. Some Bible students believe that Moses himself either wrote or collected most of the books of Genesis, Exodus, Leviticus, Numbers, and Deuteronomy.

The first reference to a book as such is found in 2 Kings 22 and 23. Hilkiah, during the renovating of the Temple (621 BC), reported to King Josiah, "I have found the book of the law in the house of the Lord" (22:8). Because of the religious reforms that followed, most scholars believe that the book discovered was at least the major portions of our present Deuteronomy. Genesis, Exodus, Leviticus, Numbers, and Deuteronomy form our present Pentateuch, the bedrock foundation of Israel's faith. Late Judaism attributed the entire work to Moses whose spirit, religious genius, and mission dominated the whole narrative and meaning of the Pentateuch. That traditional designation permeates the New Testament.

Later the Prophets and the Writings were placed with the Pentateuch. The entire Old Testament vibrates with the dynamic encounter of Israel with God. In contrast to all other religious literature of the time, the Bible preserves God's written, inspired Word as an authentic authoritative account of God's revealing and redeeming acts in preparation for the coming of Christ.

In similar fashion, certain books of the New Testament also indicate that they grew out of earlier oral and written material. So Luke stated in the introduction to his Gospel:

> Inasmuch as many have undertaken to compile a narrative of the things which have been accomplished among us, just as they were delivered to us by those who from the beginning were eyewitnesses and ministers of the word, it seemed good to me also, having followed all things closely for some time past, to write an orderly account for you, most excellent Theophilus, that you may know the truth concerning the things of which you have been informed (Luke 1:1-4).

Luke told us he had made a careful investigation of the gospel from eyewitnesses and many written records so he could provide a more complete and orderly account of Jesus' life. With much the same kind of introduction, his second volume (Acts 1:1 *ff.*) preserves our only historical record of how the gospel began to make its way into all the world.

The living stream of biblical history with its dynamic literature carried through into the second century of our era. Each book of the Bible came out of the covenant communities of faith, Israel and the church. While we do not know the names of every human writer of the Bible, it conveys the overpowering impression that God is the singular Author who inspired them.

The Bible as Holy Scripture.—Both Old and New Testament writers constantly use the phrase "it is written," indicating the special veneration ascribed to God's written Word. The entire Old Testament was frequently referred to as "the Scriptures." Often the terms, *holy, sacred,* and *divine* are attached to the word *Scripture,* or *Scriptures.* The term is older than either the word *canon* or *Bible* to refer to those holy writings in which God's will and purpose are made known.

The Formation of the Old Testament Canon

The Law Became Scripture

Biblical research reveals that, during the Exile, bereft of Temple and land, Israel came to attach more and more importance to her sacred literature. It is believed by many that the scribal priests, custodians of Israel's sacred writings, are the ones responsible for preserving, editing, and compiling the Old Testament writings as we now have them.

The first collection to receive authoritative recognition was the Pentateuch. Many Old Testament scholars today believe that the Pentateuch as we now have it is the compilation out of many strands of tradition, written laws, and other material, showing the masterful work of later editors.[3] However, some scholars believe that Moses was the sole author or main source of the Pentateuch. What is known for certain is that after the return from the Exile, about 444 BC, the Pentateuch became the first portion of the Bible accepted as a canon of Holy Scripture, though some scholars give the later date of 367 BC.[4]

Ezra is generally credited as the one responsible for preserving and bringing from Babylon the sacred scrolls of Israel. Nehemiah 8 records how Ezra (called both a scribe and a priest) read from the "book of the law of Moses" over a period of several days in which Levites and others interpreted its meaning to the assembled people. Subsequent Israelite history confirms the fact that from this time onward the Pentateuch was accorded special veneration as the written Word of God, always standing above all other books in authority.

When the Samaritans broke away from the Jews, resettling in Judea about 400 BC, they took only the Law with them, further confirming the fact that at this time only the Pentateuch was considered Holy Scripture. It was the first portion of the Hebrew Scripture to be translated into the Greek of the Septuagint, sanctioned by Ptolemy II, called Ptolemy Philadelphus, king of Egypt from 285-246 BC. Throughout Jewish history, no other portion of the Old Testament was ever accorded equal authority with the Law.

The Prophets Became Scripture

The second portion of Hebrew scrolls to be added to the canon was the collection of the prophets. It consisted of two parts: the Former Prophets of Joshua, Judges, Samuel, and Kings; and the Latter Prophets in two divisions: the Major Prophets of Isaiah, Jeremiah, and Ezekiel, and the Minor Prophets (so called because their books were shorter than the Major Prophets) designated the Twelve, one scroll containing Hosea, Joel, Amos, Obadiah, Jonah, Micah, Nahum, Habakkuk, Zephaniah, Haggai, Zechariah, and Malachi.

From the prophetic viewpoint, the Former Prophets interpreted Israel's history from the conquest to the release of Jehoiachin, king of Judah, from prison in Babylon, about 561 BC (2 Kings 25: 27-30). They recount the place and influence of some of the earlier important prophets in Israel, such as Samuel, Nathan, Gad, Micaiah, Elijah, and Elisha.

Two apocryphal books report the Jewish tradition that Ezra and Nehemiah were instrumental in preserving the sacred scrolls of Israel. Second Maccabees says of Nehemiah that he "gathered together the acts of the kings, and the prophets, and of David, and the epistles of the kings concerning the holy gifts and sacrifices" (2:13).[5]

Second Esdras reports the fanciful legend of how Ezra over a forty-day period reproduced ninety-four books. Twenty-four correspond to our Old Testament canon. The other seventy reflect the rich diversity of Hebrew literature, delivered to the wise to be read in private.

It was the general belief during the time between the Old and New Testaments that the living voice of prophecy had died out with Malachi. No book written after that, about 450 BC, was to be admitted to the collection of the prophets. Jesus, the son of Sirach, listed the Former and Latter prophets as we know them about 180 BC. His grandson, about 132 BC, three times refers to the "Prophets" as the second part of a threefold canon.[6]

By the time of the persecution under Antiochus Epiphanes (175-

164 BC), who had decreed the destruction of the Hebrew Scriptures, the Prophets had been added to the canon of Holy Scripture.

The Writings Became Scripture

The third group of material to be added to the canon of the Old Testament was simply called "The Writings." It was composed of both ancient and later material: Psalms, Proverbs, Job, Song of Songs, Ruth, Lamentations, Ecclesiastes, Esther, Daniel, Chronicles, and Ezra-Nehemiah. Due to differences in taste and subject matter, disputes over certain books lasted for generations, namely Ezekiel, Jonah, Proverbs, Song of Songs, Esther, and Ecclesiastes. The inclusion of the last three in the canon was debated into the third century AD.

New Testament writers usually refer to the Hebrew Scriptures as the "law and the prophets" (Matt. 5:17; 7:12; Luke 16:16; Acts 13:15), indicating that, while known, the Writings were not then accepted as part of the canon. Earlier references to a threefold collection of sacred writings indicate, however, that they were well on their way in being so considered. Luke 24:44 mentions the Psalms as part of Scripture. This verse could reflect the acceptance of the Writings as Scripture by some.

The Council of Jamnia

Following the destruction of the Temple in AD 70, the village of Jamnia near Jaffa became a center of Jewish learning. There, in a council held either in AD 90 or 118, the scribes of the Pharisees dealt with several practical matters affecting the Jewish community. Chief among them was to settle on an accepted Hebrew canon. The Christians had taken over the Septuagint as their Holy Scriptures. The Septuagint contained certain "outside books" which the rabbis firmly rejected, namely the Apocrypha.

The value of some books would still be debated into the third century AD. But for all practical purposes, after the Council of Jamnia, the Hebrew canon was closed. The Hebrew canon consisted of the thirty-nine books in its threefold divisions of the Law, the Prophets, and the Writings. Long since accepted as Holy Scripture, over a period of centuries since the return from the Exile, these books

alone emerged out of a vast array of literature as the authentic witness
to God's redeeming presence in Israel.

As G. R. Driver aptly comments, "The intrinsic worth of the books
so selected under divine guidance caused them to be recognized as
authoritative Scripture and needed no human agency to insure their
veneration."[7]

The Books Left Out

The "outside books" rejected by the Jamnia rabbis are generally
classified as the "Apocrypha" and the "Pseudepigrapha." The term
apocrypha means "hidden books," in the neutral sense of designating
those books not suitable for public worship, but restricted to the wise.
Pseudepigrapha means "writings under assumed names" and mainly
of an apocalyptic nature, filled with symbolic imagery setting forth
God's judgments and promised intervention and deliverance of His
people, of which three may also be found in the Apocrypha.

The Apocrypha consists of: Epistle of Jeremy; 1 Esdras; Tobit;
Ecclesiasticus; The Song of the Three Holy Children; Judith; Prayer
of Manasses; Additions to Esther; Susanna; Bel and the Dragon; 1 and
2 Maccabees; The Wisdom of Solomon; Baruch; and 2 Esdras.[8]

The Pseudepigrapha consists of: Enoch, The Sibylline Oracles; Testaments of the Twelve Patriarchs; Jubilees; 3 and 4 Maccabees; The
Psalms of Solomon; Assumption of Moses; Slavonic Enoch; The Syriac Apocalypse of Baruch; Testament of Abraham; Ascension of
Isaiah; Apocalypse of Abraham; Apocalypse of Moses; Greek Apocalypse of Baruch; and the Book of Joseph and Asenath.[9]

Written between 200 BC and AD 100, these books were rather
widely read and circulated both among the Jews of Palestine and those
of the Dispersion. The Law and the Prophets were already clearly
accepted as canonical Scripture. The Writings were in a state of flux,
although Proverbs, Psalms, and Job were beginning to be accepted as
holy books. The Apocrypha was scattered among the books of the
Septuagint Greek translation, later to be widely used among the
Christians.

After the fall of Jerusalem in AD 70, when it was apparent the
expectations of the apocalyptic writers failed to materialize, the "outside books" came under heavy censure by the Jews in Palestine. Their
occasional use by the Christians was another factor prompting the

Council of Jamnia to designate what books were to be accepted as a final canon of Hebrew Scriptures. However, Ecclesiasticus survived into the twelfth century, even quoted by some later rabbis as Scripture.[10]

Nevertheless the "outside books" have a special historical value in helping us to better understand the thought-world of the intertestamental period that led up to the Christian era. Their influence can even be detected in some books of the New Testament. For example, Jude apparently quotes from Enoch and makes an allusion to the assumption of Moses (Jude 9,14). Reading these books may also increase your appreciation for the Bible.

The Formation of the New Testament Canon

The gospel, God's good news of saving grace in Jesus Christ, began to make its way into the world through the preaching of the apostles. Christians inherited the Hebrew canon (in the Septuagint translation from Alexandria) as their first sacred Scriptures. In time, the Christian community found it necessary to have its own distinctive canon of sacred writings. The process was similar to that which produced the Old Testament canon. "The New Testament books probably were written from about AD 51 or 52 until the last decade of the first century, about a half century in all. Recognition of some came early and for some only after a long period of testing and usage. The New Testament canon was largely settled by AD 200, but not until the fourth century was there anything like general agreement for the whole New Testament."[11]

The Need for a Written Witness

How soon gospel material came to be written down we cannot tell for certain. The Gospels give no indication that any disciple wrote anything during the lifetime of Jesus, and we know He Himself left nothing in writing. The early church historian Eusebius, bishop of Caesarea (about 260 to about 340), reported that Papias, bishop of Hierapolis in Asia Minor in the second century, recounted how Matthew "put in order the oracles (or sayings) of the Lord in Aramaic, which each one interpreted as he was able."[12] That Matthew could have done this during Jesus' lifetime is possible, but we have no sure evidence that he did so at that time.

Papias also reported that Mark, after Peter's death, "committed to writing what he remembered from Peter's recollections of the Lord—accurately, but not in order."[13] Luke's Gospel reveals that earlier narratives (probably including Mark) were used by Luke as he sought to compose a more orderly account of Jesus' life (1:1-4). Several factors contributed to the growing need for a written witness to God's final revelation in Jesus Christ.

To preserve the oral witness.—The preaching of the gospel existed in a fluid form as the various apostles dispersed from Jerusalem with the message of God's saving grace provided in Jesus Christ. According to the needs and special interests of the various Christian communities as they came into being, narrative incidents out of Jesus' life, His sayings (Matthew's oracles?), miracles, and parables seemed to have circulated in "bits and pieces," as it were (Luke 1:1). The passion account (the last week in Jerusalem recalling Jesus' teaching, His Passover meal in the upper room, His arrest, trial, crucifixion, and resurrection) was the heart of the preaching. It was interpreted from the Old Testament how a crucified Messiah was nevertheless the fulfillment of God's promise and purpose despite the Law's injunction, "cursed be every one who hangs on a tree" (Gal. 3:13; Deut. 21:23).

Essentially the preaching of the gospel centered on the cross as God's power and wisdom (1 Cor. 1:23). Very early the preaching became fixed in form, as can be gathered from Luke's report of apostolic preaching recorded in Acts (Acts 2:14-39; 3:13-26; 4:10-12; 5:30-32; 10:36-43; 13:17-41). Paul's letters also reflect traditional material passed on to him, including some of the teachings of Jesus (1 Cor. 15:1-7; Rom. 1:1-4; 8:24; 10:8-9).

The four Gospels were written to record the testimony of the apostles and other eye-witnesses (Luke 1:2). The authenticity of these Gospels was to be later clearly distinguished from certain false gospels.

To confront the world with the message.—As Christianity spread, it became necessary to have reliable written material for the instruction of new converts and to provide a reliable history of the life of Jesus in witnessing to the Gentiles. Very early the letters of Paul began to be circulated and read in worship services. Selections from the Old Testament and the Gospels also were read for this purpose.

To combat heresy.—Before the close of the first century, certain heretical tendencies began to show up, calling for an authentic apostolic answer. John's Gospel, the First Epistle of John, and Colossians reflect controversy with the Gnostics who denied the reality of the incarnation. Heresies of the second, third, and fourth centuries played a decisive role in prompting the church finally to settle on an authoritative canon of New Testament writings.

Delay of Christ's return.—As the second coming of Christ seemed more and more remote, the writings of the apostles provided stability and hope to the Christian community. Paul dealt with the problem in his Thessalonian letters, and John's Gospel takes the delay into account as well (John 21:20-23), stressing the continued presence of Christ through His Spirit. Second Peter, though long disputed, nevertheless encourages patience that God will yet keep His promise, reminding Christians of Paul's same admonitions on the same subject (3:4-16).

The death of the apostles.—As the apostles, who hoped Christ might return during their lifetime, died, the necessity to preserve a written record of their witness became all the more urgent. As their living voices became silent, their writings filled the void with a permanent authoritative interpretation of the facts and meaning of the life of Jesus as God's final and complete revelation of Himself. In contrast to many false gospels written later, the four canonical Gospels of Mark, Matthew, Luke, and John alone bore the marks of material that could be traced back to dependable eyewitnesses.

As the Pentateuch became the foundation of Israel's faith, so the four Gospels became the foundation documents for the church.

The Canon of the New Testament

The Bible of the early church.—From the beginning, the first Christians had the Greek translation of the Old Testament called the Septuagint. It also contained a number of books from the Apocrypha. The Septuagint was the most often quoted translation by the New Testament writers, who considered it the inspired Word of God.[14]

As the gospel spread throughout the Mediterranean world where Greek was the common language, the Septuagint became the most readily usable Scripture for the missionary task of the church. Paul habitually used it as he went first to the Jewish synagogues in the cities he visited on his missionary journeys. After it was rejected by the rabbis of Jamnia as too much a Christian book, Aquila, a Jewish convert from Pontus, produced in AD 128 a Greek translation for the Jewish community. In AD 245 Origen completed the Hexapla in which he compared the Hebrew text with four different revisions of the Septuagint out of his scholarly concern for the many translations of the Greek text that differed from that of the Hebrew.

The collection of Paul's letters.—The oldest writings of the New Testament are the letters of Paul, written sometime between AD 50 and 63. Metzger lists them chronologically in four groups each with its special theological concern.[15] The first are the two letters to the Thessalonians dealing with eschatology, the doctrine of last things. The next group contains Galatians, 1 and 2 Corinthians, and Romans, with chief emphasis on the doctrine of salvation. These are followed by Ephesians, Colossians, Philippians, and the personal note to Philemon, stressing the doctrine of Christology on the person and work of Christ. The final group contains the Pastoral Letters to Titus and the two to Timothy with instructions on the duties of the pastor in providing church leadership. (Many scholars believe the Pastorals were written by a disciple of Paul based on genuine notes from the apostle himself.)

Written in the main to churches Paul had established on his missionary journeys, his Letters provide the most extensive and profound interpretation of the gospel to be found in the New Testament. The letters also deal with the practical problems of church life and the moral and spiritual issues of the Christian life.

They are intensely warm and personal, and it is evident that Paul intended them to be shared by the various churches. He gave specific instruction to the church at Colossae that it be done. "When this letter has been read among you, have it read also in the church of the Laodiceans; and see that you read also the letter from Laodicea" (Col. 4:16).

Paul wrote out of a sense of authority derived from Christ Himself. "For you know what instructions we gave you through the Lord Jesus" (1 Thess. 4:2). "So then, brethren, stand firm and hold to the traditions which you were taught by us, either by word of mouth or by letter" (2 Thess. 2:15). "Now we command you, brethren, in the name of our Lord Jesus Christ" (2 Thess. 3:6). He wrote out of a sense of the inspiration of the Holy Spirit or as a direct command of Christ (1 Cor. 2:13; 14:37).

Second Peter 3:16 places Paul's letters on a par with other Scriptures. When and by whom Paul's letters were collected for distribution, we cannot tell. Evidence is clear, however, that by the end of the first century numerous churches had some or all of his letters. Many scholars believe that traces of Pauline thought and language are to be found in John's Gospel, James, 2 Peter, and the letters of John.[16]

To have Paul's letters read in Christian worship along with passages from the Old Testament indicates how the Christian community was moving in the direction of having its own distinctive canon of sacred writings.

Early collections of the New Testament books.—Almost immediately upon their composition, the Gospels became widely distributed. They are referred to in their fourfold form by a number of the early church fathers. The seven letters of Ignatius, bishop of Antioch in Syria written while on his way to martyrdom under Trajan (AD 98-117), make references to the authority of the Gospels.

Justin Martyr (AD 110-165) quoted almost exclusively from our Gospels. Eusebius and Origen refer to the four Gospels. Theophilus of Antioch (about AD 170) was the first to quote the New Testament as inspired Scripture along with the Old Testament prophets.[17] The second letter of Clement actually cites the Gospels as Holy Scripture (about AD 150).

By the middle of the second century, the church had at its disposal a vast body of written material—letters, apocalypses, apologies, instruction manuals, and acts of the apostles—composed after the death of the apostles. Among such were the Gospel of Peter, the Preaching of Peter, the Apocalypse of Peter, the Acts of Peter and John, for example, later to be rejected by the church as unworthy of the canon.

Marcion, the Gnostic heretic from Pontus, was one of the first to conceive the idea of a proper list of Christian Scriptures. He appeared in Rome about AD 150 with his "official list." He completely rejected the Old Testament as picturing a God inferior to the One revealed by Jesus. In place of the Law, he put the Gospel of Luke purged of all its Jewish elements. For the Prophets, he substituted ten letters of

Paul, whom he claimed to be the promised Holy Spirit. For the Writings, he placed his own work, the Antitheses, showing how, in his opinion, the New Testament contradicted the Old Testament.[18]

The response of the church was swift and decisive as evidenced by the so-called Muratorian Canon dated around AD 170 and named after L. A. Muratori who discovered it. It is a Latin translation containing the four Gospels, Acts, 1 and 2 Corinthians, thirteen epistles of Paul, 1 and 2 John, Jude, and Revelation, as well as two books later rejected, the Apocalypse of Peter and the Wisdom of Solomon. The books omitted, James, 2 Peter, 3 John, and Hebrews, are the very ones that took longer to be accepted.

About the same time, Montanus, who claimed to be the Holy Spirit with new visions of revelation, also prompted the church to give its sanction only to those books considered apostolic. Origen (AD 182-251), the leading scholar of Alexandria for fifty years, traveled extensively in Rome, Greece, Asia Minor, Egypt, and Palestine to evaluate what books the various churches considered authentic. He discovered opinions varied as to which were acknowledged, disputed, or false.

Eusebius of Caesarea (AD 270-340) made a similar study, being the first to mention the General Epistles. He also spoke of Jude, James, 2 Peter and 2 and 3 John as disputed, with some doubts about Revelation. Among the spurious books, he listed the Acts of Paul, the Shepherd of Hermas, the Apocalypse of Peter, the Didache, and the Letter of Barnabas.

Early in the fourth century, Cyril of Jerusalem and Gregory of Nazianzus agree on twenty-six of our twenty-seven, excluding the Revelation. "The earliest known list of New Testament writings corresponding exactly our twenty-seven, no more and no less, appeared in the Easter letter of Athanasius, bishop at Egypt, in AD 367."[19] These books were approved by a local council convened at Hippo in 393 and later at the Third Council of Carthage in 397, at which Augustine was present. The Third Council of Carthage decreed that "apart from the canonical scriptures, nothing may be read in the Church under the name of divine scriptures."[20] This was the only time a church council formally ruled on the canon. Not until the Reformers of the sixteenth century raised some questions about the disputed books did the question about the canon seriously arise again.

It can be safely concluded, therefore, that by the end of the fourth century the canon had been closed for the Western branch of the church.

The church and the canon.—The proposition that since the church created the canon the church alone has the right to proclaim authoritative interpretations of Scripture was seriously challenged by the Reformers. The question of scriptural authority over the traditions of the church was a central issue for them. Deciding on a canon was simply the church's recognition of those authentic apostolic writings which had molded and guided the church in its formative stages. The canon was determined more by the self-evident power of the books selected than by any formal decision either by church or council.

The books left out.—In addition to the books later judged to be truly apostolic, a vast body of other literature was written in the early years of Christianity. Various ones were accepted as Scripture by different church leaders as evidenced by their presence in some of our oldest existing copies of the New Testament.

One group of writings was collected together as the Apostolic Fathers and contained: 1 and 2 Clement, the Epistles of Ignatius, the Epistle of Polycarp to the Philippians, the Martyrdom of Polycarp, the Didache (also called "The Lord's Teaching to the Gentiles by the Twelve Apostles"), the Letter of Barnabas, the Shepherd of Hermas, and the Epistle to Diognetus.

Another group sometimes called "The New Testament Apocrypha" consisted of spurious works written in the names of the apostles and others. These claimed to supply information about Jesus and the apostles not found in the canonical Scriptures. Gospels were written in the names of Mary, Joseph, Marcion, Philip, Bartholomew, Peter, Matthew, and Thomas. One such gospel tells the story of how Jesus at age five made sparrows out of clay on the sabbath and clapped his hands, whereupon the birds came alive and flew away singing.[21]

Other books were written as the Acts of Andrew, Barnabas, James, John, Paul, Peter, Philip, Pilate, Matthias, and Thomas. Other books were apocalypses in the names of James, Paul, Peter, Thomas, Stephen, and the Virgin.

Lacking the "ring of truth," the church wisely rejected all of these false works. In reality, by their very nature, they excluded themselves from the canon eventually adopted.

The Apocrypha of the Old Testament has enjoyed a checkered career in the church through the centuries. Tertullian, Irenaeus, Clement, and Origen accepted the Apocrypha as part of the Christian Bible, as did Augustine, though recognizing their difference from the Hebrew text. Cyril of Jerusalem (died 386) and Jerome (died 420) were the first to apply the term *Apocrypha* to these books, though as a scholar Jerome found it necessary to include them in his Latin translation of the Vulgate. Augustine's view was most generally accepted throughout the Middle Ages until the Reformers broke with the Roman church.

Luther was the first to collect the apocryphal books in one place in his German translation of 1534. While useful for reading they were not held equal for doctrinal purposes as was true in the Roman Church which declared them canonical at the Council of Trent (1546) and later confirmed by the Vatican Council of 1870.[22] Protestant and Evangelical churches follow the judgment of Luther in rejecting the Old Testament Apocrypha as inspired Scripture.

What is remarkable in the formation of the Christian Bible is how our present sixty-six books have emerged out of a vast store of ancient literature. It seems to me that the doctrine of inspiration must be deep and broad enough to include not only the writing of the original books but must include the recognition of the Spirit's guidance as well in the collection, transmission, translation, preservation, and final selection of the present books making up our canon of Holy Scripture.

Standards of Selection for the Canon

Many formidable factors compelled the church to reach a decision about an acceptable canon of Scripture: Heretic Marcion supported a shortened canon; Montanus and other charismatics were making wild speculations; the Gnostics claimed apostolic authority for their philosophical speculations; and more false gospels, acts, epistles, and apocalypses were circulating. Three basic tests were applied for a book to be included in the canon.

Wide acceptance in the church.—Only those books were selected that had been in use for a long time by many churches. Such usage confirmed the fact that the books were early recognized for their value as true witnesses to the faith.

Christian nurture in the church.—The worth of a given book was measured in terms of its authentic witness to the life and teachings of Jesus. In comparison, the false gospels, full of fanciful stories and wild imagination, could not hold their own against the canonical Gospels. The fact that many heretics also based much of their doctrine on some of them further hastened the rejection of such books. Books that also served to nurture the faithful in doctrine and Christlike living proved their worth long before they were included in a canon of Scriptures.

Earmarks of apostolic authority.—The most important standard for selecting a book was its evidence of being from an apostle, to whom it was known Christ had committed His message. The writers showed evidence that the Spirit that inspired the Old Testament writers was present in them as well. If not written by an actual apostle, it had to be shown that the writer had derived his material from an apostle or another eyewitness to the life of Jesus. Thus Mark and Luke were accepted because tradition affirmed that behind them stood the preaching and teaching of Peter and Paul.

For a while 2 Peter, Jude, James, Hebrews, the Revelation, and 2 and 3 John were doubted until apostolic connections were finally attested for them. Though accepted as an apostle "born out of due time," Paul's letters rang with apostolic authority from the beginning. Their doctrinal content and value for Christian nurture were never in doubt.

Eventually every book selected had behind it apostolic authority in some manner. The material in each book came out of the lifetime of Jesus or during the lifetime of the apostles themselves. Following the apostles' deaths, it became all the more imperative that the church preserve and treasure what came from their hands. While some other books came into existence during the lifetime of the apostles, and many others in the centuries before the church finally decided on a New Testament canon, only those demonstrating the earmarks of genuine apostolic witness were eventually accepted.

Did the apostles write any other books not contained in our New Testament? Whether by an apostle or not we do not know, but Luke referred to many who had compiled narratives (Luke 1:1) before he wrote his Gospel. He assured us they came from eyewitnesses. Literary research on Luke's Gospel reveals that Mark may have been one such source used by him. He referred to other writers as "ministers of the word," thus bearing genuine apostolic authority. Some scholars believe that material common only to Matthew and Luke (sometimes designated *Q* from the German *quelle,* "source"), may have been drawn from a written document compiled by an unnamed apostle from the circle of the first disciples of our Lord. Many scholars believe that collections of "testimonials" containing narratives and teaching material from Jesus' ministry and used in the first preaching of the gospel began to circulate early.

The canonical Gospels do not claim to give us an exhaustive and complete account of everything Jesus ever said or did. What they do claim is to give us the basic essentials for an accurate account of how Jesus as the promised Messiah, the eternal Son of God, has fulfilled the preparatory revelation of the Old Testament, through whom God offers eternal life to all who believe in Him.

Thus John in his Gospel wrote, "Now Jesus did many other signs in the presence of his disciples, which are not written in this book; but these are written that you may believe that Jesus is the Christ, the Son of God, and that believing you may have life in his name" (John 20:30-31). He then closed his Gospel with a final reminder that his account had been purposely selective in its witness to Jesus, "But there are also many other things which Jesus did; were every one of them to be written, I suppose that the world itself could not contain the books that would be written" (21:25), assuring us that his testimony to Jesus is true (v. 24).

How many other letters Paul may have written we cannot tell. His Corinthian letters indicate that there were others written to Corinth. In Colossians, he referred to a letter to the Laodiceans (Col. 4:16) which we do not have, unless, as some scholars believe, the Ephesian letter was the original Laodicean epistle, since the superscription, "The Letter of Paul to the Ephesians," was added later. The best copies of the letter itself make no reference to Ephesus.

As we follow the process by which the canon was finally approved, it seems providential that enough time elapsed to allow the books selected to prove their worth. That was especially important in light of so many false gospels, acts, letters, and apocalpyses which were beginning to distort the apostolic witness.

Barclay summarized the stages of development most clearly:

It has to be written, it has to be widely read; it has to be accepted as useful for life and for doctrine; it has to make its ways into the public worship of the Church; it has to win acceptance not simply locally but throughout the whole Church; and finally it has to be officially approved by the voice and decision of the Church.[23]

Underlining all these factors was the major one of true apostolic authority. Although the Reformers later would again raise the question of the true worth of those books the early church also disputed, namely, the Revelation, James, Jude, 2 Peter, 2 and 3 John, and Hebrews,[24] there was no intention to exclude them from the canon.

It is impossible to imagine that another list of books out of the vast literature of the first four centuries of the church could provide as authentic a witness to Christ and the apostles as our present canon, and certainly not superior to them. While some churches include other books in their canon, all accept the twenty-seven books listed by Athanasius (AD 367) as the bedrock foundation of authoritative apostolic witness to God's final revelation of Himself in Jesus Christ.

Paul reminded us that the church is "built upon the foundation of the apostles and prophets, Christ Jesus himself being the chief cornerstone, in whom the whole structure is joined together and grows into a holy temple in the Lord" (Eph. 2:20-21).

In the New Testament canon, we have God's own inspired witness to that foundation.

Notes

1. Alexander Souter, *The Text and Canon of the New Testament* (London: Duckworth, 1948), p. 154.

2. Edwin Lewis and David G. Downey, eds., *The Abingdon Commentary* (Nashville: Abingdon Press, 1929), "The Transmission of the Old Testament," Ira M. Price, p. 101.

3. The reader is referred to the more scholarly works which set forth the history of research on the Pentateuch. For example: *A Companion to the Bible,* T. W. Manson, ed.; *The Abingdon Bible Commentary,* F. C. Eislen, Edwin Lewis and David G. Downey, eds.; William Barclay, *The Making of the Bible;* and the excellent article in *The Encyclopaedia Britannica,* Volume 3.

4. T. W. Manson, *A Companion to the Bible* (Edinburgh: T & T Clark, 1946), pp. 42, 76.

5. William Barclay, *The Making of the Bible* (Edinburgh: The Saint Andrew Press, 1951), p. 27f.

6. *Abingdon Bible Commentary*, p. 94.

7. *Abingdon Bible Commentary*, p. 98.

8. Manson, pp. 80-89.

9. Ibid., pp. 89-96.

10. *The Interpreter's Dictionary of the Bible* (New York: Abingdon Press, 1962), I, pp. 162-163.

11. Ralph Herring, Frank Stagg, and Others, *How to Understand the Bible* (Nashville: Broadman Press, 1974), p. 130.

12. *The Interpreter's Dictionary of the Bible*, 3, p. 648.

13. Ibid.

14. Bruce Manning Metzger, *The New Testament, Its Background, Growth and Content* (Nashville: Abingdon Press, 1965), p. 216.

15. Ibid., p. 218.

16. Barclay, p. 67.

17. Ibid., p. 74-75.

18. Ibid., p. 80.

19. Herring, Stagg, and Other, pp. 132-133.

20. *The Interpreter's Dictionary of the Bible*, 1, p. 531.

21. Metzger, p. 101.

22. *The Interpreter's Dictionary of the Bible*, 1, pp. 164-165.

23. Barclay, p. 64.

24. Ibid., p. 90.

5
Beyond the Sacred Page

Introduction

Written in faraway lands, in a language not our own, arising out of a society so different from ours, how does the Bible speak to us in our time, our language, our culture? Accepted as God's written Word of revelation and redemption, how does God speak to us through its sacred pages? On what basis do we ascribe to it a unique and final authority relevant to modern people as God's continuing revelation of Himself? How are we to understand its meaning for those to whom it first was written? Are any passages no longer relevant for us? Is the Bible merely a handbook on moral instruction? Is it a blueprint for all future events unfolding in history? What is the relationship of its abiding truths to all other kinds of knowledge and truth? What is its meaning for us today?

Such questions as these raise the problem of interpretation, which has to do with understanding the original meaning of the text and its meaning for later generations. The various books of the Bible are themselves interpretations of God's mighty acts of revelation and redemption as "men moved by the Holy Spirit spoke from God" (2 Pet. 1:21).

The Science of Hermeneutics

The science or method of interpretation is called hermeneutics. It is derived from the Greek, *hermēneuo,* "to express, to explain, to translate, to interpret." This Greek word is often used in the New Testament to explain Aramaic or Hebrew words (John 1:38; 9:7; Heb. 7:2; John 1:42). Another form of the verb means "to search, to look into," as in John 5:39: "You search the scriptures, because you think that in them you have eternal life; and it is they that bear witness to me." The compound verb is found in Luke 24:27 with the meaning "to explain thoroughly," in the Emmaus account, as the risen Lord "beginning with Moses and all the prophets, he interpreted [*diērmēneuo*] to them in all the scriptures the things concerning himself."

The last two references illustrate the basic clue of interpretation throughout the New Testament: The apostles interpreted the Old Testament in terms of its witness to Jesus as the Christ who fulfilled the promises of God.

Two Basic Disciplines

Biblical interpretation involves two basic disciplines, exegesis and exposition. Exegesis comes from the Greek, *exēgeomai,* meaning "to unfold in teaching, to recount, to declare." In John 1:18, it is used of Christ's revelation of God. "No one has ever seen God; the only Son, who is in the bosom of the Father, he has made him known."

Basically, exegesis has to do with the interpretation of the original meaning of a text. Exposition, meaning "to explain, to put forth," builds on exegesis to show the contemporary relevance of the text, without falsifying its original sense. Thus, together, exegesis and exposition deal with the two main focuses of biblical interpretation, its original meaning and its present relevance and application.

Biblical interpretation grows out of one's understanding of the nature of the Bible, one's view of inspiration and revelation, and one's concept of the Bible's authority. One's understanding of the nature of reality and truth, and how truth is to be verified, must also be taken into account. The proper relationships of faith and reason are important elements in biblical interpretation as well.

Two basic approaches to the above matters are usually taken, one philosophical and the other biblical. The philosophical approach brings *to* the Bible already held ideas about reality, truth, and the meaning of human existence derived from rational speculation. It provides its own categories and thought patterns through which the biblical message is to be expressed and understood. The biblical approach derives *from* the Bible itself the basic categories, terms, thought patterns, and understandings through which the unique message of the Bible is best understood. The two approaches are often mixed together, as the history of interpretation reveals. This is especially true when the gospel is addressed to the world outside the Bible wherein other truths of God are also to be found.

While founded on exegesis (the original meaning of a text), the ultimate goal of interpretation relates the meaning of the text to readers of each generation. God encounters us and addresses us through His written Word. Both aspects of interpretation take into account the particular cultural situation in which God addresses His people: Exegesis explores in the original cultural context the particular needs of the situation at the time; exposition draws out from the original text the abiding truths of God's will and purpose as applied to a new and ever-changing cultural situation.

While our cultural situation changes from age to age, our moral and spiritual nature remain the same, especially our need of redemption. Since redemption is the ultimate aim of revelation, and since the Scriptures were given to "make [us] wise unto salvation through . . . Christ Jesus" (2 Tim. 3:15, KJV), the Bible not only tells us what God said to those of old, providing for their salvation, but also remains God's continuing address to us through which His saving grace is now available to us.

The Bible not only tells us what God said a long time ago but also helps us understand how God speaks to us in our time and situation. God's word includes more than just the Bible. Nevertheless, the Bible provides the key and clue for understanding what He is saying presently in the created order (Ps. 19; 104; Rom. 1:20), in the moral judgments of history (Amos 1—3), in our own moral conscience (Rom. 2:14-16), and in the church (Rev. 2—3).

Biblical interpretation is most true to the Scriptures when it concentrates on the message of salvation centered in Jesus Christ as the Word made flesh. He is the major key that unlocks all the hidden treasures of the Bible. Through His own Holy Spirit, God interprets to us Jesus as the Christ and the risen Lord through whom we are "changed into his likeness from one degree of glory to another" (2 Cor. 3:18).

He was called Jesus (Yahweh saves) for He came to save His people from their sins (Matt. 1:21). In Him God's love was enfleshed, His mercy incarnated, His grace overflowed, His salvation embodied. To know that, to receive that mercy, to be filled with that love, and to know you are forgiven is to know and experience the meaning and intention of Scripture. Interpretation is aimed at making known the reality of God's saving grace.

History of Interpretation

Nearly two thousand years of biblical interpretation have revealed a variety of approaches and changing principles in the field of hermeneutics. Such changes became necessary as knowledge of biblical languages and the history and culture of biblical times have vastly increased. For the scholar and the lay reader alike, it is helpful to know something of the history of interpretation.

The Tradition of Judaism

Believing the living voice of prophecy to have ceased with the last of the prophets (Malachi?), there grew up alongside the Old Testament an extensive body of oral law. One tradition held that the oral law had been handed down from the time of Moses through a line of scribes who became its teachers and guardians.[1] A stronger tradition held Ezra to be the "father of the oral law." It was a growing body of rabbinic interpretation in several parts, known as the Mishna ("to repeat," to learn by memorizing), in contrast to written Scriptures learned by reading.

The oral law was highly thought of as a necessary "hedge about the Law" and claimed by the scribes to be the authoritative interpretation of the Scriptures. It was in reference to the oral law that Jesus asked, "And why do you transgress the commandment of God for the sake of your tradition?" (Matt. 15:3), and commented, "So, for the sake of your tradition, you have made void the word of God" (v. 6). Whereupon He quoted Isaiah 29:13 against the Pharisees and scribes:

> "This people honors me with their lips,
> but their heart is far from me;
> in vain do they worship me,
> teaching as doctrines the precepts of men"
> (vv. 8-9).

The motive for the oral law was to provide a continuing revelation adapting the written Law to changing times. Its various parts were finally written down in the fifth century AD in two editions known as the Talmud, one in Babylon and the other in Jerusalem. Throughout the Middle Ages and into modern times, the Talmud continues to be a basic textbook in Jewish schools and for the orthodox the source of the guiding principles for the new state of Israel.

Rabbi Hillel (the Elder, about 60 BC-AD 20), some scholars believe he may have been one of the doctors questioned by the boy Jesus (Luke 2:46-47), developed seven rules of exegesis: 1) light and heavy, from easy to difficult; 2) equivalence of similar passages; 3) from special to general; 4) inference from many passages; 5) from general to special; 6) analogy from several passages; and 7) inferences from the context.[2] Other rabbis later expanded these rules into thirteen, thirty-two, and forty-nine rules.

The story is recorded that Rabbi Shammai, a contemporary of Hillel, rebuked a proselyte who asked to be taught the whole law while standing on one foot. The proselyte then approached Hillel who told him, "What is hateful to thee do not do to thy fellowman; this is the whole Torah; all else is commentary."[3] Jesus taught the more positive responsibility, "So whatever you wish that men would do to you, do so to them; for this is the law and the prophets" (Matt. 7:12).

While much in the oral law provided practical wisdom for understanding how to live by the Scriptures, the overall weight of the interpretations became grievously burdensome. Such was Jesus' concern in His repeated woes pronounced on the scribes and the Pharisees (Matt. 23:4). While growing out of a noble motive to be true to God's Word, the end result was an overemphasis on the form of words, the letter of the Law, the exaltation of outward appearance and ceremonial, and a "holier-than-thou" attitude of self-righteousness. More was made of fringes and phylacteries (a leather box containing the Shema tied with knots that formed the name of God, Yahweh, and worn on the forehead as a charm, Num. 15:39; Deut. 6:8; Matt. 23:5)[4] than the weightier matters of the Law—justice and mercy (Matt. 23:23). In contrast to those who believed people were created in order to keep Torah, Jesus condemned this type of Phariseeism in His statement, "The sabbath was made for man, not man for the sabbath; so the Son of man is lord even of the sabbath" (Mark 2:27-28).

Though occasionally addressed as Rabbi (Teacher), and standing in the tradition of Judaism, Jesus' interpretation of Scripture breathed a whole new air of freedom from the burdens of the oral law. In Him God's Word was once again alive with saving power. "The crowds were astonished at his teaching, for he taught them as one who had authority, and not as their scribes" (Matt. 7:28-29).

Paul exhibited for us the best example for what became for all New Testament writers the major key for the interpretation of holy Scripture: Christ as the fulfillment of the preparatory revelation in the Old Testament. Many passages, however, reflect Paul's rabbinic schooling at the feet of Gamaliel "according to the strict manner of the law" (Acts 22:3). Following his conversion, rabbinic methods of exegesis were used for the single purpose of interpreting Christ as the preexistent Son of God, the promised Messiah, and risen Lord. His exegesis was thoroughly Christ-centered.

Paul came to see the Old Testament in a completely new light. He quoted freely from the Septuagint which he considered to be the inspired Word of God (2 Tim. 3:16). Paul occasionally used typology, allegory, and the symbolic meaning of individual words to expound God's revealing presence in the life, death, and resurrection of Jesus Christ. Although Paul was influenced by his rabbinic training, his approach to Scripture showed a new freshness of interpretation of the Old Testament Scriptures.

According to Paul, "Christ is the end of the law, that everyone who has faith may be justified" (Rom. 10:4). He warned us that the "written code kills, but the Spirit gives life" (2 Cor. 3:6). Thus the Spirit opens our eyes to the true meaning of Scripture.

The manner in which Jesus, Paul, and the other New Testament writers interpreted Scripture provides the basic principles of exegesis and exposition for interpreting both Testaments. Emphasis is laid on the function and purpose of Scripture, "For whatever was written in former days was written for our instruction, that by steadfastness and by the encouragement of the scriptures we might have hope" (Rom. 15:4). They are written to make us "wise unto salvation through faith which is in Christ Jesus," (2 Tim. 3:15, KJV), that He may dwell in our hearts by faith as our "hope of glory" (Col. 1:27). The Spirit is promised as Counselor and Teacher to make Christ known (John 14:26; 16:12-15).

Interpretation in the Early Church

In the early years of the church, certain principles of interpretation soon made themselves apparent. Two centers of Christian scholarship, Alexandria in Egypt and Antioch in Syria, became representative of two approaches to biblical interpretation. Among others two issues required special attention: the relation of the Old Testament to the New Testament and the relationship of the gospel to the world of Hellenistic philosophy.

Clement of Alexandria (150?-213) became an early champion of typology as a method of exegesis relating the two sets of documents. Typology understands that persons, events, and things in the Old Testament prefigure persons, events, and things in the New Testament which have revelatory significance. The historical interrelationship was that of promise and fulfillment.

Clement discerned five possible meanings of Scripture: (1) the historical; (2) the doctrinal; (3) the prophetic; (4) a philosophical; (5) the mystical.[5]

Alexandria became noted for the method of allegory for which Origen (185?-254?) was chiefly noted. In allegory the plain meanings of the words are bypassed for the supposedly deeper, hidden, spiritual meaning for which the words of the text are merely symbols. Earlier the Greek philosophers had used allegory to explain the otherwise crude and obscure meanings in Homer and other Greek literature. Allegory was also used to offset the extreme literalism of the Gnostics and the followers of Marcion who rejected the Old Testament. Philo of Alexandria had used allegory and Platonic philosophy to demonstrate how Moses had anticipated the Greek philosophers.

Origen developed a threefold sense of Scripture: the literal, the moral, and the spiritual, corresponding to his understanding of human nature as composed of the body, soul, and spirit.

The school of Antioch reacted against what became for it the excesses of allegory and sought to interpret Scripture according to grammatical-historical principles. Antioch put most emphasis on the human element in the Bible and the historical reality of revelation. Its chief exponent was John Chrysostom (345?-407), the greatest preacher of the ancient church.

Despite the differences, both schools had much in common: Scripture was the inspired Word of God, though not by dictation; God had accommodated Himself to human ways of thinking and speaking; and the chief end in interpretation was to proclaim salvation in Jesus Christ.

Embracing the above principles, Augustine (354-430) is best noted for his famous maxim: "I believe in order that I may understand." His basic position through exegesis was to put faith above reason, based on Isaiah 7:9, "Unless you believe, you shall not understand" (based on the Latin translation).

Augustine's interpretation of the parable of the good Samaritan is one of the most famous examples of the use of allegory: the man was Adam; Jerusalem, the heavenly city; Jericho, the man's mortality; thieves, the devil and his angels; man was stripped of his immortality; priest and Levite, the priesthood and ministry of the Old Testament; Samaritan, the Lord Himself; the beast, Christ's incarnation; the inn, the church; the morrow, the resurrection; and the innkeeper, the apostle Paul.[6]

Believing philosophy to be the handmaiden of theology, Augustine employed Platonic concepts in the interpretation and proclamation of the gospel. Augustine's basic exegetical methods prevailed into the Middle Ages, as did the fourfold sense of Scripture from the apostolic fathers: (1) the literal (historical); (2) the allegorical (mystical); (3) the anagogic (eschatological); and (4) the tropological (the moral).[7]

Because Augustine's approach to Scripture dominated the exegetical methods of the church for a thousand years, it is well to bear in mind certain other principles of interpretation used by him. Diligent Bible study should result in increased love for God and one's fellowman. While Scripture admits of several levels of meaning, the spiritual sense, which is understood mainly through allegory, takes precedence over the literal. In confrontation with heretical sects, Augustine appealed to the authority of the church's *regula fidei,* the rule of faith.[8] (Already Irenaeus and Tertullian, two other early church leaders, had set the example for such an appeal.) As a means of communicating the gospel to the Hellenistic thought-world, Augustine embraced the philosophy of Plato with its concept of eternal ideas, especially the idea of God innate in the human mind, whereby knowledge of reality was derived by deduction from the general to the particular.

Interpretation in the Middle Ages

Usually reckoned as the years between the fifth and fifteenth centuries, the Middle Ages produced a system of Christian doctrine known as Medieval Scholasticism. The philosophy of Aristotle replaced that of Plato and reason replaced faith as the basic approach to biblical interpretation.

In the ensuing years, the doctrines and traditions of the church became more rigidly fixed. The church, as the guardian of Scripture and the teaching of the early church leaders, assumed the exclusive right to impose the only proper interpretation of Scripture by authoritarian decree. The tendency toward a rigid and absolute dogmatism began in the early Christian centuries, chiefly to protect the faith from heretical teachings.

Beginning as simple baptismal confessions, the rule of faith came to fuller expression in the Apostle's Creed and later came to include the creedal confessions of the early church councils. Augustine, Irenaeus, Tertullian, and Ambrose all appealed to the authority of the church as set forth in the rule of faith. Gregory the Great (who became pope in 590) claimed full and equal dogmatic authority for the Scriptures (the four Gospels), church tradition, and the creeds of Nicea, (325), Constantinople, (381), Ephesus, (431), and Chalcedon, (451).[9] Vincent of Lerins (434) defined the criteria for Catholic orthodox doctrine as that which has been "believed always, everywhere, and by all."[10]

Through the Dark Ages, the seventh to the twelfth centuries, and the Scholastic Era, the twelfth to the sixteenth centuries, exegesis of the Scripture was confined to the sterile and unprogressive repetitions of church dogma. The teachings of the church were set forth in numerous Catenae (catena, "link"), a chain of quotations from the church fathers. The prevailing motive was to prove the reasonableness of the faith.

The direction toward scholasticism was set by Anselm's *Cur Deus Homo?* (Why the God-man?), by rational argument, to prove the church's dogma to Christians, Jews, and Gentiles alike. This rational approach was advanced by Abelard (1079-1142) in his comparisons of the fathers. He was concerned by reason to resolve the contradictions between Scripture, the fathers, and church decrees. In his *Sic et Non* (Yes and No), he weighed the different authorities by rational evaluation, believing reason could not contradict revelation and holding to the final authority of the Bible. He saw a distinction between important and unimportant elements in Scripture, thus anticipating Luther.[11]

Peter Lombard's "Four Books of Sentences," consisted mainly of quotations from the Latin fathers, Ambrose, Hilary, and Augustine. His book became the major textbook of scholasticism along with the *Summa Theologiae* of Thomas Aquinas (died 1274).

By the start of the thirteenth century, all the works of Aristotle became known in the West. The translations of his works by Boethius (480?-524?) helped to enthrone Aristotelian logic as the basic method to organize and systematize Christian doctrine as a body of knowledge interpreted by human reason.[12] So thoroughly did Aristotle become accepted that "in 1629 the Sorbonne decreed that to contradict Aristotle was to contradict the church," and Erasmus held that to reject Aristotle would be the end of the Christian religion.[13]

Scholasticism reached its definitive expression in the great work of Thomas Aquinas (1225-1274), whose approach to doctrine was clearly philosophical. Like the schoolmen before him, he sought to relate reason to faith. By Aristotle's method of induction, whereby all knowledge arises out of the five senses, Aquinas set forth his famous fivefold proofs for the existence of God accessible to human reason, which formed the foundation of his two-storied structure of theology. The upper story was the revelation given in Scripture for man's salvation. Reason and revelation were the two paths to a knowledge of God.

Aquinas moved away from allegorical speculation and put more emphasis on the grammatical-historical, literal meaning of Scripture.[14] While still holding to the multiple sense of Scripture, he put reason above faith, which by Aristotelian logic conceived faith to be more a matter of a system of ideas derived from Scripture.

Scholastic theology, however, was not without its critics. Chief among its opponents were the monastics, best exemplified by Bernard of Clairvaux (1090-1153) who deemphasized the place of reason in religion. He rejected the scholastic position based on reason, "I understand that I may believe." He modified Augustine's position, "I believe that I may understand," with his emphasis on a form of mystical, experiential theology that held "I believe in order to experience."[15] The monks spent their time in copying manuscripts, and Bible study was carried on in an atmosphere of prayer and devotion until the mystical experience of God became an end within itself.

Returning to Augustine's stress on the primacy of faith, other theologians raised their voices against the arid theology of the Scholastics, namely, John Duns Scotus (1265?-1308?) and William of Occam (1285?-1347). For both, Scripture and church tradition were primary authorities over rational arguments. Occam went so far as to separate science (reason) and theology, in which he championed Scripture alone against the teachers of the church.

Breakthrough in the Reformation

Opposition to the church's authority began to arise in the thirteenth century. Contact with Arabian culture and the Greek classics through the Crusades brought a new impetus to learning which became evident in the growth of the universities of the West. The study of the more complete works of Aristotle encouraged greater interest in the natural sciences. Nationalism began to challenge the exclusive claims of the church. In the name of genuine piety, the corruption of the Papacy was being questioned as never before.

Among the forerunners of the Reformation, special attention must be given to John Wycliffe (1330?-1384) and John Huss (1374-1415). Wycliffe challenged the authority of the popes as unscriptural and the view that church tradition was equal to the Bible. He returned to Augustine's position that faith leads to understanding, and the Bible is an all-sufficient source of doctrine. He called for dependence on the Holy Spirit and the spirit of love and humility as essential in the study of the Bible.[16] He laid great stress on the saving message of the Scriptures whose truth was plain enough for the common reader.

Influenced by Wycliffe, Huss chiefly objected to the view that made the decrees of the popes equal to the Scriptures, and his methods of exegesis won the praise of Luther.

The revival of learning occasioned by the Renaissance added its voice of protest to the ecclesiastical and feudal despotism of the late Middle Ages, thus marking a transition to the modern age. The rebirth of interest in the philosophical and cultural ideas of the Greco-Roman world created a new intellectual concern that created new approaches to literature, science, art, and architecture that spread throughout Europe. The new spirit of inquiry helped fan the flames calling for the reformation of the church and its teachings. A whole new way of looking at reality, truth, and the rights and values of

human nature found expression in new approaches to biblical interpretation as well.

But the reformation of the church awaited the coming of a man
strong enough in mind and spirit, and perceptive in understanding, to
penetrate to the heart of the church's deepest need—a return to a truer
understanding of Scripture and its central message of salvation. That
man was Martin Luther!

The full extent of Luther's work as the great reformer is beyond the
scope of this present work. We can only give attention to the central
highlights of his treatment of Scripture in summary fashion.[17] Luther's teachings were hammered out on the anvil of controversy with
the church over a period of years, resulting in the ninety-five theses
posted on the church door at Wittenberg on October 31, 1517. In all
his protests, Luther appealed to Scripture which he considered to
possess superior authority over all church decrees and the traditions
of the church.

Luther soon abandoned the medieval exegesis of the fourfold sense
of Scripture in favor of a single meaning based on the natural, grammatical sense of a passage. His major key of interpretation was to find
Christ everywhere in Scripture. The true spiritual sense was no longer
to be found in allegory but in the message of salvation centering in
Christ as God's living Word. The authority of Scripture was in its
revelation of Christ and its function to provide salvation in Him alone.

Luther clearly recognized the human element in the Bible and
approached the text on the basis of God's accommodation to human
ways of speaking and writing. He distinguished between what he
considered important and less important books and passages. God's
Word incarnate in Jesus was appealed to as an analogy of the human
and divine elements of Scripture. He likened the Scriptures to the
swaddling clothes and the manger in which Christ had lain.

Luther felt free to question the relative value of certain books of the
canon. He had serious questions about Esther, Jeremiah, Job, the
Song of Songs, Jonah (which the early rabbis had also questioned),
Revelation, Jude, Hebrews, and James. For him Paul's Epistles contained more gospel than Matthew, Mark, and Luke. Romans, Galatians, John, and 1 Peter were considered the "kernel and marrow of
all books." While holding to the inspiration and authority of the Bible

as a whole, he was able to recognize that certain passages and books spoke more clearly of salvation than others.

He protested the view that the pope and the priests were to be the sole interpreters of Scripture. The Holy Spirit was promised to all believers and recognized that the word *priest* was never used in the New Testament of Christian ministers. He believed that the message of salvation was plain enough for all people to read the Scriptures for themselves, prompting him to translate the Bible into the German language.

Christ Himself is the object of faith and not intellectual assent to the dogmas and traditions of the church. Salvation, therefore, is a matter of "justification by faith" and founded on the grace of God alone and not good works. Luther made a clear distinction between law and gospel: law revealing sin and our need for salvation and the gospel providing the grace of redemption. Dependence on the Holy Spirit is an essential for understanding Scripture.

In revolt against arid Scholasticism, Luther decried the ability of natural, unredeemed reason to lead persons to God. While reason is valid for discovering truths about the world, only when led by faith can it aid in the study of Scripture. He spoke of philosophy as the "enemy of God" and the "devil's whore" and of Aristotle as that "pagan beast" and the "destroyer of pious doctrine," so strongly did he protest scholastic theology.

Farrar summarizes Luther's exegetical principles as follows: (1) the need for grammatical-historical knowledge; (2) attention to the context; (3) faith illumined by the Spirit; (4) Scripture interpreting Scripture; (5) Christ as the key and clue.

As a general rule, Luther did not consider the Apocrypha as canonical Scripture. He was the first to collect it in one place which he published between the two Testaments in his German translation. However, on one occasion he considered Ecclesiasticus as holy Scripture. Not as final authority but as helpful guides to interpreting Scripture, Luther accepted the creeds of the early church councils because they were in agreement with the New Testament. He consistently challenged the pope's authority and traditional church dogma as being equal to the Scriptures.

For Luther, the Bible was not a textbook on all kinds of knowledge. Its central content was the message of salvation in Jesus Christ. He made a clear distinction between science and philosophy on the one hand and faith and Scripture on the other. Theology and science dealt with two separate spheres of reality.

Luther's exposition of all Christian doctrines was founded on the Scriptures. He did not ascribe scientific and technical accuracy to the form of biblical words and never ceased to wonder that, in accommodation to our human weakness, God was able to communicate His saving revelation through imperfect human speech.

Luther's exegesis of Scripture grew out of his deeply felt personal need for assurance in salvation. The question he addressed to the Bible was, How can I find a gracious and saving God?

The three cardinal teachings for which Luther is most widely remembered go to the heart of his reforming principles: *Sola scriptura* —Scripture alone. Against all other authorities, especially the papal decrees and church tradition, he set the final, supreme, and all-sufficient authority of Scripture. Amid all the frailty of its human form, the Bible's central message of salvation could be plainly understood in which "there is no falsehood." The function of Scripture is not to give us scientific and philosophical truths but "to make us wise unto salvation in Jesus Christ."

Justification by faith alone was God's unique work in Christ on our behalf. No human merit by works of righteousness could avail to put us in right standing with God. Luther protested against the sale of indulgencies of the Roman Catholic Church. Webster's dictionary defines indulgencies as the "remission of part or all of the temporal and esp. purgatorial punishment that according to Roman Catholicism is due for sins whose eternal punishment has been remitted and whose guilt has been pardoned." This forgiveness was obtained at that time in history by the payment of money. To Luther indulgencies were falsely based on the Church's doctrine of doing penance, as prescribed by the priests. Luther believed penance was a distortion of the New Testament teaching on repentance. God's grace alone, provided in the atoning death of Christ, appropriated by personal faith in Christ, was the sole means of salvation. Good works were to be an expression of the redeemed life and were totally inadequate as the basis of justification.

The priesthood of every true believer annulled the necessity of making confession to human priests. Through the Holy Spirit promised to every believer, one need confess only to God directly. Luther made no spiritual distinction between laity and clergy, which led to no distinction between the secular and the sacred. Distinctions in the church were distinctions of office and function for the sake of order and teaching. It meant also that everyone must be free to read and interpret Scripture through the guidance of the Holy Spirit. It meant also that every true believer was "a priest at his neighbor's elbow" to hear confession and offer pastoral comfort and encouragement to one's brethren.

With emphasis on Christ as the living Word, in the hands of Luther the Scriptures came alive with saving power. His exegesis and biblical interpretations pointed the way of deliverance from the dry and overintellectualized orthodoxy of scholastic theology.

Trained as a lawyer and schooled in the Christian humanism of the Renaissance, John Calvin (1509-1564) became the greatest exegete and theologian of the Reformation.[18] The great Swiss Reformer agreed with many of the major points of Luther, though sharp divisions also existed between them, especially over baptism and the Lord's Supper.[19] Other differences pertained to the doctrine of the church and the relation of church and state, though both held theoretically to the separation of the two.

Our chief interest here is their agreement on the doctrine of Scripture. Scripture, as the inspired Word of God, exhibits a superior authority over the doctrines, decrees, and traditions of the church. It is our only source of a true knowledge of God, all-sufficient for faith and the Christian life. Calvin warned against interpreting Scripture as having any other function than to reveal Christ for our salvation.[20]

Calvin also approached Scripture with the principle of accommodation as a major clue for interpreting the Bible. He made a distinction between the content of Scripture (Jesus Christ for our salvation) and the style and form of the words, which reflected God's own accommodation to our human ways of speaking and writing. As did Luther, he used the analogy of Christ's incarnation for understanding the human and divine elements in Scripture. Calvin's training in the critical analysis of ancient classical literature enabled him to approach the Scriptures with the same historical appreciation for the cultural setting of the biblical writers. He rejected the idea that rational proofs of the Bible's divine authority were first necessary before one could believe its message of salvation. Though believing in verbal inspiration, in contrast to Luther, Calvin nevertheless recognized technical errors in the text whose inconsistencies in no way obscured the essential message of salvation, but recognized such as God's accommodation to our human ways of understanding.

Calvin put much emphasis on the inner testimony of the Holy Spirit by which Scripture was able to authenticate itself. He rejected as foolish the attempt of reason to prove Scripture to be the Word of God, for only through faith "does Scripture suffice to give a saving knowledge of God when its certainty is founded on the inward persuasion of the Holy Spirit."[21]

For Calvin, the Bible was not a textbook on science. The biblical writers spoke in the idiom of the times and described nature in phenomenological terms (as nature appeared to the naked eye), which was also a form of God's accommodation. Anthropomorphic passages were considered in the same light. Though conditioned by the cultural context in which they wrote, both Calvin and Luther believed the biblical writers were free from error in their communication of the message of salvation.

Though differing from one another in many respects, the great Reformers—Luther, Calvin, and Zwingli—were in basic agreement on the supreme and all sufficient authority of Scripture for faith and living the Christian life. The voices that for a hundred years had been calling for the reformation of the church found in the Reformers able spokesmen and writers.

The dark side of the Reformation was to show itself in the doctrinal controversies that raged for generations to follow, often mixed with political conflict as well. Nor were the Reformers without their faults, as witness Luther's suppression of the Peasant's Revolt and Calvin's consent to the execution of Servetus. But all was a sincere attempt to expound and preserve the purity of the faith as witnessed in the many great confessions of faith set forth in the following centuries. The movement could not be stopped, and all grew out of a return to the Scriptures.

As controversy continued unabated, within a hundred years after Calvin, the Post-Reformation theologians resorted more and more to a defensive position that led straight into a form of Protestant Scholasticism, as discussed in chapter 2. The refreshing prophetic insights of the great Reformers were replaced by the spirit of the ancient scribes and Pharisees. Orthodoxy came to be measured more and more in terms of intellectual assent to new rigid definitions. For the first time in Christian history, the effort was made to define the manner of inspiration. Supernatural verbal dictation was considered necessary to ensure the infallibility of the inspired writers. The principle of accommodation, dating back to Augustine, was ignored and more emphasis was placed on the form of the words than on the message of salvation they were meant to communicate. The Bible became a textbook on all kinds of knowledge, leading to literalistic and legalistic interpretations of Scripture that all but ignored the human element in the Bible so clearly discerned by Calvin and Luther.

Farrar describes the new Protestant Scholasticism as follows: "The Reformation soon parted company with free learning, turned its back upon culture, held out no hand to awaking science, and lost itself in a maze of theological controversies."[22]

The Counter Reformation in the Roman Church came to official expression in the Council of Trent (1545-1563). Its major decrees, in opposition to the Protestant Reformation, dealt with Scripture and tradition, sin, grace, justification, and the sacraments. For the first time, the church declared its traditions to be equal in authority with the Scriptures, defined the canon as including the Apocrypha with the Vulgate (dating back to Jerome's Latin translation of the fifth century) as the official text, and declared the church to be the only authoritative interpreter of Scripture, thus laying the groundwork for the doctrine of the pope's infallibility when speaking *ex cathedra* (in matters of faith and morals only) as declared by the Vatican Council of 1870.[23]

But the Reformers had opened up a whole new approach to biblical interpretation that would continue and flourish in the modern period. We turn now to describe some of the more important aspects of biblical research that provide special guidance in biblical interpretation.

Modern Research and the Bible

From the sixteenth century to the present, biblical research has expanded into several specialized fields of inquiry. Rules used to analyze the classical literature of ancient Greece and Rome, learned in the Renaissance, came to be applied to the literature of the Bible. As a result, new theories on the nature of history and interpretation were applied to biblical studies. Scholars of eighteenth century Germany took the lead in this, but their work also influenced biblical studies in England and America.

While much good came out of this kind of research, not all of the conclusions of the German critics[24] were widely accepted. Conservative scholars pointed to the danger of approaching the Bible as if it were only another book. Some conservatives reacted to the excesses of German scholars by rejecting any of the new approaches to biblical study. Other conservatives, however, felt that careful study and research pose not a threat but a challenge to those who approach the Bible as inspired and authoritative. Three areas of modern biblical research have proved helpful in interpreting the Bible.

Textual Research

Since we do not have any of the autographs (the original writings of the biblical authors), we are confined to the study of copies of copies that have accumulated throughout history. Textual research seeks to recover texts as close to the originals as possible.

Concern for the purity of the text dates from the time of Ezra, following the return from Babylon. The Jewish community was particularly concerned with the Septuagint and its many differences from the Hebrew text. This was also a chief concern of Origen, one of the earliest textual scholars. His *Hexapla* (sixfold) compared four editions of the Septuagint with the Hebrew and its Greek transliteration. He took special note of the many variations in the Greek texts of the New Testament known to him.

Jerome (340-420), the most learned biblical scholar of the Latin church, traveled to Palestine to study manuscripts for his Latin translation of the Scriptures. Jerome's translation became known as the Vulgate. The early church fathers were all aware of the variations in the manuscripts known to them.

The most extensive research on the text has been carried on by Christian scholars regarding the New Testament. Manuscripts of the New Testament, in whole or in part, number over 5,000.[25] Material available for study falls into several categories: (1) Papyrus fragments, of which P52, containing John 18:31-33,37-38, is the oldest copy of any portion of the New Testament, dating from the first half of the second century. The most valuable papyruses are the Chester Beatty collection in the Dublin Museum discovered in Egypt in 1930-1931 and the Bodmer collection in Geneva discovered in 1955-1956; (2) 266 uncials, written in capital letters on vellum (skins of cattle, sheep, goats, and antelope) from the third to the tenth centuries; (3) 2,754 minuscules, written in cursive, dating from the tenth century; 4) ancient versions in Syriac, Latin, Ethiopic, and Coptic; 5) quotations from the church fathers; and 6) ancient lectionaries, Scripture selected for public worship.[26] Some 500,000 variant readings have been catalogued so far.[27] Only fifty manuscripts contain the entire New Testament.

Following are the most important of the ancient manuscripts: *Codex Sinaiticus,* discovered by Tischendorf on his third visit to the monastery of St. Catherine at Sinai in 1859. Through delicate negotiations, he persuaded the monks to present the manuscript as a gift to the czar of Russia, patron protector of the Greek Church. Following the revolution of 1917, the USSR, in need of money, sold the manuscript to the British Museum for $500,000.[28] It is the only known complete copy of the Greek New Testament in uncial writing. It contains most of the Old Testament, all of the New Testament, the Epistle of Barnabas, and the Shepherd of Hermas.

Codex Alexandrinus, containing the Old Testament with some mutilations and most of the New Testament, was presented to King Charles I of England by the Patriarch of Constantinople in 1627. It is now on display in the British Museum and dates from the fifth century. *Codex Vaticanus,* in the Vatican Library since 1475, dates from the fourth century and contains all of the Apocrypha except Maccabees. *Codex Ephraemi* is a palimpsest (to rub clean). Having erased the Scripture text, a twelfth-century scribe copied thirty-eight sermons of St. Ephraem from the fourth century. With chemical reagents Tischendorf recovered the original portions of the Old and New Testaments underneath, which revealed corrections made by scribes in the sixth and ninth centuries, the original dating from the fifth century.

Theodore Beza presented a manuscript dating from the fifth or sixth century to Cambridge University in 1581. The manuscript is now known as the Beza manuscript. Written in Greek and Latin, it contains most of the four Gospels, Acts, and a portion of 3 John. It contains more variations than any other known manuscript.[28]

Published in 1516, the reconstructed Greek text by Erasmus was destined to become the *Textus Receptus* (the received text) in England through the publication by Stephanus of Paris, who, in 1550, reproduced Erasmus' fifth edition of his own text in 1535.[29] Thus, Erasmus's text became the foundation text of the King James translators of 1611. The discovery of superior texts after the sixteenth century show that Erasmus was limited by inferior copies. In the last four hundred years, many other editions of the New Testament have been published, giving rise to the many new translations in our own time.

One of the most interesting discoveries of textual research is the five different endings for the Gospel of Mark. The longer ending (16:9-20) appears in a Syriac version of the second century and appears in Greek manuscripts only after the fifth century. The ancient church fathers, along with Jerome, comment on its absence in most of the copies known to them.[30] Its vocabulary and style differ from the rest of the Gospel. It is generally agreed that the longer ending was added by a later copist.

The 500,000 variations studied, however, in no way affect the basic saving message of the Bible. No scholar claims that we have succeeded in reproducing an exact copy of the autographs, though "it is a seldom disputed fact that critical science has to all intents and purposes recovered the original text of the New Testament."[31]

Literary Research

Using the best text available, literary research deals with the questions of authorship, date, place of writing, sources, style of writing, and the purpose of the author.

One of the most difficult areas of such study has been the analysis of the four Gospels, but the results have been most rewarding. The Synoptic Gospels of Matthew, Mark, and Luke in their extensive agreement in content, arrangement, and wording reveal a literary dependence that cannot be ignored. Upon close examination, we discover that 90 percent of Mark appears in Matthew and 53 percent of Mark appears in Luke. Matthew and Luke contain 235 verses common to both but not found in Mark. It is assumed that both had access to some common source, whether written or oral we cannot tell, from which they drew this material. This source has been designated *Q* (from the German *quella*—source) by scholars.

In addition, Matthew has 300 verses found only in his Gospel, while Luke has 520 verses not found elsewhere.[32] Matthew and Luke used their material from Mark in different ways, but both followed Mark's basic outline. The analysis bears out Luke's introduction that he used many sources, some written, some oral, to give us a more orderly and complete account of Jesus' life (Luke 1:1-3). Most scholars assume that Matthew's Gospel was composed in much the same manner. God's Spirit, of course, worked in and through this process to achieve His purpose.

Many other differences appear in Matthew and Luke which suggest that each had his own purpose in presenting his material in the way he did. Matthew was concerned to indicate how Jesus fulfilled the Old Testament in his many quotations from it. He collected the sayings of Jesus in five sections accompanied with appropriate narrative material: discipleship (3:1 to 7:29); apostleship (8:1 to 11:1); kingdom of God (11:2 to 13:52); the church (13:53 to 19:2); eschatology (19:3 to 26:1). Matthew was the Gospel most often quoted by the church fathers and was widely used for instruction of new converts in the early church.

Luke, the Gentile, stressed Jesus' special interest in women, children, and the "outcasts" of Jewish society. Tracing Jesus' genealogy back to Adam, Luke emphasized Jesus as the Savior of all humanity.

The style of John's Gospel differs markedly from the Synoptics. It is more theological in tone, and Jesus' discourses are given in long passages which develop particular themes. John stressed Jesus' encounters with a select list of individuals. He gave independent accounts of Jesus' ministry in Judea and Jerusalem. He did not report the baptism or the cry of dereliction from the cross. He reported the cleansing of the Temple early in Jesus' ministry. Given at various times in the Synoptics, John reported the titles used of Jesus all in his first chapter: the Word of God, the Lamb of God, Rabbi, the Messiah, King of Israel, Son of God, and Son of man.[33]

These are but a few examples of the data examined by literary research. They aid us in understanding the rich variety of style, emphases, and theological purposes expressed by the writers of the Bible.

Literary research also studies the language of the Scriptures and the possible forms of the oral witness that preceded the written accounts. Also studied is the life-situation in the early church that helped shape the final form of the gospel witness.

Not all scholars, however, are in agreement with all the findings of literary research. Many conclusions must remain in the area of theory and tentative judgments, as the research continues. But intellectual honesty requires us to listen with open and prayerful minds and to come up with better answers if we disagree. As a human book, the literature of the Bible can be studied with the same rules of research applied to other ancient literature. But as also a divine book, the unique nature of the Bible as a record of God's revealing and saving deeds in history must be the major key in its interpretation.

Historical Research

This method is also called the historical-literary method because it is concerned with dates, sources, persons, and places. It is important to know something of first-century Judaism and the Greek world into which Christianity moved. This method examines the history of Israel and the church in the context of the history and culture of the people surrounding them. It is helpful to know as much as we can about the history, religion, and thought-world of ancient Babylon, Egypt, Canaan, and the Greco-Roman world through which God's community of faith moved. Ancient documents, inscriptions, and artifacts uncovered by archaeology become extremely valuable in this regard.

An examination of how certain words, concepts, and ideas were used in these cultures helps us better to understand how they were used in Scripture. For example, the grandeur of Israel's account of the creation is best understood against the background of the ancient creation myths of Babylon. Knowing something about emperor worship helps us to understand why the early Christians proclaimed Christ alone as Lord and why they laid down their lives for their faith.

Historical research helps us distinguish between the abiding truths and principles found in Scripture and the cultural setting in which they first were given. An example is Paul's admonition against eating meat sacrificed to idols. The abiding principle is Christian love and consideration for others. Paul's exhortation to "obey the higher powers" in Romans 13 is a different setting than the situation of John in Revelation.

Jesus' cleansing of the Temple has its own peculiar setting, not likely duplicated in our lives, but the principle remains—worship must be pure, free from all crass commercialism, and idolatry must be cleansed from the heart. Yet its truth as a revelation of Jesus' messianic sovereignty remains. The new content Jesus poured into such terms as *Son of God, Son of man,* and *Messiah* must be seen against their use in the Old Testament.

The most serious question raised by historical research has to do with the meaning of history itself. By their very nature, past events are unrepeatable. The historian cannot reproduce them to see what happened, as a scientist can reproduce an experiment in the laboratory to see what can happen. The study of past events is confined to the investigation of the documents and records that tell of the event. One of the most important facts of the event is the interpretation of the meaning of the event by those who were involved in the event. The historian may give his own meaning of the event in the light of the consequences that follow from it, but he cannot change what it meant to its original participants.

Later interpretations may draw out more of the meaning of a past event than it was possible to understand at the time of the event. So it was that the disciples understood some things only after the resurrection (John 2:22). The letters of Paul are another example of how a fuller understanding of Jesus was only possible later under the teaching of the Holy Spirit, even as Christ had promised (John 16:12-15).

To conceive of history as a closed system of unbroken cause and effect and to approach Scripture with a bias as to what can or cannot happen is to misunderstand the nature of biblical faith. Biblical faith is belief and trust in the living God who is Lord of nature and history. To be most helpful, historical research into the Scriptures must take into account the Bible's unique view of history. The biblical reality is that God has been, and is, at work for our redemption. Secular historians can neither prove nor disprove the incarnation and the resurrection; both are realities beyond the reach of scientific investigation whose meaning for salvation can be confirmed by faith alone.

The biblical writer was more concerned to tell us the meaning of an event, as faith discerned God's presence in it, than to give an objective description of the bare facts as might have been given by any unbeliever. Faith, therefore, is an essential ingredient of an event and is itself a fact to be reckoned with. How important faith is for understanding the biblical witness may be discerned in scholarly works of the nineteenth century which are known as "the quest of the historical Jesus."

Some scholars recognized that the Gospels are not simple biographies in the modern sense of the word. The Gospels are the faith-interpretations of those who believed in Him as the Messiah, the Son of God and the Savior of the World. Some scholars assumed that the early church changed the simple teachings of Jesus into something different than Jesus taught; in other words, they made a distinction between the "historical Jesus" and the "Christ of faith." They assumed that, if one could lay aside temporarily the disciples' faith in Jesus, one could get at a truly unbiased description of the "real" Jesus of history. One of the presuppositions of the quest was the assumption that the disciples had imposed their own view on who Jesus was.

The nineteenth century produced many "lives of Jesus," with varying and disappointing results. The effort to be merely a neutral observer of the historical Jesus produced portraits of Jesus that turned out to be more the weak reflections of the liberal ideas of the scholars. The "Jesus of history" could not be separated from the "Christ of faith."

There is a new "quest of the historical Jesus," but scholars today have tried to learn from the mistakes of earlier ones. The new "quest of the historical Jesus" in our own time seeks better to understand the ingredient of faith in order to grasp the real meaning of Jesus as the Christ. It refuses to stumble over the "claim of Scripture"—that "God was in Christ, reconciling the world unto himself" (2 Cor. 5:19, KJV) and truly raised Him from the dead. It takes seriously that history involves a dimension of reality that only faith can grasp, that lies beyond the ability of so called objective scientific research to comprehend.

Historical research into Gospel origins, however, requires us to reinterpret some of the imagery of the biblical thought-world. It confirms the true historical reality of Jesus which faith, by the Spirit of God, confirms as the same risen Lord of the church. Jesus is no

mere mythological being. Thus we are saved from the ancient heresy
of Docetism in which His humanity was only so in appearance.

While these highly technical disciplines of biblical research—Textual, Literary, and Historical—are the special province of those scholars particularly trained for carrying them out, we all are helped by
their devoted and careful labors. We may not always agree with the
findings and conclusions, but we should not cheat ourselves of the
value when throwing new light on biblical interpretation.

Notes

1. Frederic W. Farrar, *History of Interpretation* (Grand Rapids, Michi-
gan: Baker Book House, 1961), p. 62, "Supported by the false decretals of
Judaism which asserted that the Oral Law had been handed down by Mosaic
succession."

2. Ibid., pp. 18-19.

3. *The Interpreters Dictionary of the Bible*, 2, p. 605.

4. As late as the twelfth century, Rabbi Rashi claimed the law on fringes
to be the greatest commandment since the word *tsitsith,* "fringes," with the
eight threads and five knots equaled 613, the total number of commandments.
Quoted in Farrar, p. 50.

5. Robert M. Grant, *A Short History of the Interpretation of the Bible*
(New York: The Macmillan Company, 1972), p. 80.

6. C. H. Dodd, *The Parables of the Kingdom* (London: Nisbet and Co.,
Ltd., 1946), pp. 11-12.

7. Richard N. Soulen, *Handbook of Biblical Criticism* (Atlanta: John
Knox Press, 1978), pp. 13, 15, 73, 169.

8. Jack B. Rogers and Donald K. McKim, *The Authority and Interpretation of the Bible* (San Francisco: Harper and Row, 1979), pp. 32, 34.

9. J. L. Neve, *A History of Christian Thought* (Philadelphia: The Muhlenberg Press, 1946), pp. 136, 173.

10. Ibid., p. 148.

11. Farrar, p. 260.

12. Rogers and McKim, pp. 36-37.

13. Farrar, p. 265.

14. Rogers and McKim, p. 47.

15. Ibid., pp. 50-51.

16. Ibid., pp. 74-75.

17. The following summations are taken from the following works: Rogers and McKim, pp. 75-88; Neve, pp. 218-238; and Farrar, pp. 324-341.

18. Neve, p. 275.

19. Ibid., pp. 249-255 on the Eucharist; pp. 279-280. on baptism.

20. Rogers and McKim, p. 107.

21. John Calvin, *Institutes of the Christian Religion* (Grand Rapids: Wm. B. Eerdmans, 1957), Henry Beveridge, trans, I. VII. 23, p. 83.

22. Farrar, p. 358.

23. Neve, p. 329.

24. The name applied to those scholars who developed what came to be called the approach of Historical Criticism. The term does not mean "to find fault with" the Bible, but "to evaluate, to weigh the evidence for." But the term has acquired a negative emotional connotation that has caused undue misunderstanding. For this reason I prefer the term "research" so as to appreciate properly the better results of the method.

25. Richard N. Soulen, *Handbook of Biblical Criticism* (Atlanta: John Knox Press, 1978), p. 162.

26. Statistics taken from Bruce Manning Metzger, *The Text of the New Testament* (New York: Oxford University Press, 1980), p. 32; classifications taken from Soulin, ibid., p. 162.

27. Soulen, p. 171.

28. See Bruce Manning Metzger, *The New Testament, Its Background, Growth and Content* (Nashville: Abingdon Press, 1965), for a full description of this fascinating story, pp. 42-46.

29. Descriptions of the Codices are taken from Metzger, pp. 42-51.

30. Soulen, p. 163; Metzger, p. 102.

31. George Eldon Ladd, *The New Testament and Criticism* (Grand Rapids: Eerdmans, 1982), p. 72.

32. Ibid., p. 80.

33. Metzger, p. 83.

6
Guidelines for Biblical Interpretation

Introduction

Biblical interpretation is most true to the Scriptures when it concentrates on the message of salvation centered in Jesus Christ as the Word made flesh. He is the major key that unlocks all the hidden treasures of the Bible. Through His own Holy Spirit, God interprets to us Jesus as the Christ and the risen Lord through whom we are "changed into his likeness from one degree of glory to another" (2 Cor. 3:18).

He was called Jesus (Yahweh saves) for He came to save His people from their sins (Matt. 1:21). In Him God's love was infleshed, His mercy incarnated, His grace overflowed, His salvation embodied. To know that, to receive that mercy, to be filled with that love, and to know you are forgiven is to know and experience the meaning and intention of Scripture. Interpretation is aimed at making known the reality of God's saving grace.

Some Guidelines for Interpretation.

In our review of the history of biblical interpretation, some of the main highlights have been touched to give us some feeling for the great complexity of the process. We meet with no single universal approach in the methods used. There has been room for honest and earnest differences of opinion on many aspects of the problem of biblical interpretation. We stand on this side of the Reformation which gave us God's written Word in our own hands, in our own tongue. We have also received the abiding admonition to let the Holy Spirit be our guide and teacher to fulfill Scripture's divine intention—"to make us wise unto salvation that is in Jesus Christ."

The Problem of Literalism

One of the continuing problems of biblical interpretation is how to understand the language and the thought-world of the biblical writers. What are we to make of the prescientific view of the world reflected in some Bible passages? How are we to distinguish between early views of God from later more exalted views of God? How are we to interpret the anthropomorphic descriptions of God in Scripture?

Questions of this nature raise the problem of how literally to interpret certain passages. In most cases, the plain meaning of a word in common usage will suffice in contrast to some allegorical, mystic, or supposedly deeper "spiritual" sense. This is what is known as the grammatical-linguistic meaning, as was stressed by the ancient school of Antioch. It was used by Augustine, Tertullian, Jerome, Luther, and Calvin, for example. It is important to know the root source of words, popular idioms of a language, and the grammatical syntax used.[1]

But an overemphasis on the literal meaning of a word can lead to "literalism": the plain sense of a word, sentence, or phrase is taken at face value without regard to the writer's intended meaning. As seen earlier, the Bible contains a rich variety of literary forms. Each must be interpreted according to the purpose of the particular form being studied. Special note must be taken of the poetic passages as distinguished from the prose passages. Language is often used in a highly symbolic and figurative manner. Especially is this true of apocalyptic language as found in Daniel, Revelation, and sections in Isaiah, Ezekiel, and Mark. To interpret such language literally is to miss the theological meaning the imagery is meant to convey.

When Jesus said, "If your right eye causes you to sin, pluck it out and throw it away" (Matt. 5:29), he was speaking in figurative language. A young lady on my seminary church field took these words literally and one day took a pair of scissors and put out her right eye!

Exodus 19:4 says God brought Israel out of Egypt "on eagles' wings"; in 6:6 He did it with His "outstretched arm." The psalmist said, "The mountains skipped like rams,/the hills like lambs" (Ps. 114:4). Obviously the language is not to be taken literally, but these are examples of how vivid, figurative language is used to describe God's mighty power to deliver His people.

The tendency to take the anthropomorphic imagery of the Old

Testament literally encouraged the development of the allegorical method of exegesis in the early church. The excesses of the allegorical interpretation was one factor that prompted Marcion to discard the Old Testament completely. His rash judgment should warn us about the dangers of literalism that fail to understand the symbolic nature of much of the language of the Bible.

The more subtle danger of literalism occurs when we also fail to take into account the prescientific world view of the biblical writers. A clear example of this danger is seen in how we interpret the creation narratives.

Two accounts of creation are given in Genesis (Gen. 1 to 2:4 *a;* 2:2 *b*-25). The progressive order in the stages of creation differ in the two accounts. In Genesis 1, man and woman are created at the same time as the crown of creation after all other living things, animal and vegetable. In Genesis 2, the man is created, then the vegetable kingdom, and lastly woman. If taken as literal science, the two creation narratives seem to contradict each other. However, the creation accounts are theology, not modern science. As such, both, despite their many differences, make the same point—God as a free and sovereign Lord is the source of all life, the main point being man's true nature as created in God's image, setting forth our right relationship to God. Taken together as theology, we can rightly conclude that we have only one account of creation.

The biblical accounts of the creation deal with matters beyond the scope of science. They deal with the Who and why of creation, not the how and what. At the same time, the vivid account is couched in the limited prescientific imagery that reflects the view of the physical structure of the solar system commonly believed by the people of ancient times.

However physically conceived, throughout the Scriptures whenever the writer refers to the created order, he always stressed God's sovereignty over nature as its Creator and Sustainer. The biblical doctrine of creation stands on its own merits and its truth as revelation is not dependent on our view of the universe, whether primitive or modern.

If one makes prescientific views equal to the revelation God is making of Himself, later scientific discoveries undermine trust in the Bible as a Book of truth. Religion and science are set in false opposition to each other, forcing the unnecessary choice: modern science or revelation.

Human ways of thinking and speaking, even when found in the Bible, must not be allowed to lead us into a false literalism that obscures the eternal message of revelation and salvation.

The Original Context

To know the context of a passage of Scripture is an important principle of interpretation. The total context of a verse or passage may be likened to a series of concentric circles. The innermost circle is the actual text itself, seeing it in relation to the verses that precede and those that follow, including its relation to the book as a whole in which it is found. One asks such questions as, How does it advance the writer's thought? how is it related to what else he is saying? and, how does the passage reflect the writer's general theological outlook?

The next circle of context takes into account the life situation of the original readers, including the cultural, temporal, political, and spiritual factors in their background.[2] To know something of the cultural background of the city of Corinth as a bustling commercial center known for its moral corruption helps us understand Paul's letters to the Corinthian Christians. Knowing the political situation, the religion, and moral condition of the nations with which Israel had to deal helps us understand the prophets. The life and teachings of Jesus are best understood in the context of the religious situation of the Judaism of His day.

The still larger context of a passage is its relation to the Bible as a whole. To know where and when a particular book arose in Israel's history is to understand its special place and value in the unfolding drama of God's revelation.

Material to help us grasp the full context of a passage or book may be found in the many fine Bible dictionaries, atlases, commentary introductions, and word books now available in most book stores and libraries.

The Intent of the Writer

The more we know the full context of a passage the better prepared we are to ask about the original intent of the writer. It is safe to assume the general intent of every biblical writer was theological—he wrote under the conscious awareness that he was being guided by the Spirit of God; he wrote to proclaim the Word and purpose of God; he wrote to preserve the record of revelation; he wrote to meet the moral and spiritual needs of God's people.

The specific intent is often revealed by the context as outlined. Often the content of a passage is sufficient to reveal the writer's purpose. When Paul wrote about "the daily pressure upon me of my anxiety for all the churches" (2 Cor. 11:28), he revealed the concern that underlay the intent of each of his letters. When writing from prison in Rome to thank the Philippians for their love and care through Epaphroditus, he had the opportunity to guide them in dealing with certain tensions in the congregation.

In Galatians, Paul defended his calling as an apostle and the gospel he preached, providing an opportunity to expound on salvation by faith. Desiring to preach the gospel to those in Rome, a church he had not yet visited though he knew many in the congregation, gave Paul an opportunity to set forth the fullness of the gospel in the most carefully thought out theological treatise of the early church, and perhaps of all time.

Luke declared his intention in the opening verses of his Gospel. After researching material from written and oral sources from eyewitnesses, "having followed all things closely," he set out to "write an orderly account" (Luke 1:3) of the life and ministry of Jesus. John told us that what he had written he had written that we "may believe that Jesus is the Christ, the Son of God, and that believing [we] may have life in his name" (John 20:31). Though Mark and Matthew did not tell us in so many words, their intention was the same as that of Luke and John.

Sometimes it may be necessary to distinguish between a writer's main intent and the incidental elements found in the passage. We have already seen this in the creation narratives—the author's intent was theological, to proclaim God's sovereignty and our responsibility to our Creator and not to teach us science.

Careful attention to the literary style of a writer will often help us to understand his intention. We have seen how Matthew grouped the teachings of Jesus around five main topics; emphasis on the content of Jesus' teachings seemed more important to Matthew than reporting the actual time and place in which He said a particular thing.

The literary form and style of the Fourth Gospel is especially helpful at this point. John told us he wrote his Gospel so one may believe that "Jesus is the Christ, the Son of God" (20:31) and believing have life in His name. The way in which John wrote his Gospel is a demonstration of how one comes to that knowledge and confession. When two of John the Baptizer's disciples asked Jesus, "Rabbi, . . . where are you staying?" (1:38) "He said to them, 'Come and see' " (v. 39) which carries with it the force, "come see for yourself." The verb form for "see" has the meaning "to know through firsthand acquaintance with."

How does one come to know that Jesus the man is none other than the Messiah, the Son of God? First through the witness of those who already know who He is, which directs us to our own personal encounter of faith. One must come to see for oneself. First calling Him "Rabbi," Andrew, out of a personal encounter, confessed Jesus as Messiah then found his brother Simon who was brought to Jesus.

Philip witnessed to Nathanael that Jesus is the One promised in the Law and the Prophets (John 1: 45). When Nathanael retorted, "Can anything good come out of Nazareth?" Philip replied, "Come and see!" (v. 46). Out of his own encounter with Jesus, Nathanael made his own confession, "Rabbi, you are the Son of God! You are the King of Israel!" (v. 49).

Also by his literary style, John emphasized Jesus as the Savior of all classes and kinds of people. He did this by selecting three symbolic converts: Nicodemus a full-blooded, highborn Jew; a half-breed Samaritan woman at the well; and a possible Gentile. In each case, each "came to see" for himself or herself, also indicating the personal need and background out of which each came to know personally who Jesus is.

By his style, John also emphasized the glory of the incarnation and the progression in understanding as one encounters Jesus. John told us that, "No one has ever seen God; the only Son, who is in the bosom of the Father, he has made him known" (1:18). Through Jesus' humanity, as the eternal Word made flesh, God makes contact with our humanity. This is the beginning point in getting to know who Jesus is, but it is only the beginning. In telling about Andrew, Nathanael, the Samaritan woman, the Gentile nobleman, and the man born blind, each moved from knowing Jesus as a man to the personal confession of Him as the Messiah.

The village neighbors of the Samaritan woman are another illustration of John's "come see" theme. Having implored Jesus to stay with them two days, they then said to the woman, "It is no longer because of your words that we believe, for we have heard for ourselves, and we know that this is indeed the Savior of the world" (4:42).

The Theological Content

The major clue to biblical interpretation is to keep in mind what kind of book the Bible is. While touching on many matters of common human interest, the one central theme of the Scriptures is God's revelation of Himself. Its ultimate purpose is "to make [us] wise unto salvation . . . in Christ Jesus" (2 Tim. 3:15, KJV).

Each book has its own way of telling us what God was doing and saying among His people in that particular time in history. It is important to take note of the "many and various ways God spoke of old to our fathers by the prophets" (Heb. 1:1) in preparation for the coming of the Christ who "reflects the glory of God and bears the very stamp of his nature" (v. 3).

It is important to note that some passages reveal God more clearly than others. Through the centuries, scholars and interpreters have pointed out the necessity of allowing the clearer passages to throw light on the more obscure and difficult passages. One must keep in mind that God Himself stands behind the inspired Word and that God Himself encounters us through the written Word.

Donald G. Miller states well the theological principle of interpretation when he says, "We are making proper use of the Bible only when we are asking it questions about God, His will, His glory, and human salvation, faith and life."[3]

The Aid of the Holy Spirit

The Scripture itself teaches us to depend on the Holy Spirit for understanding the message of the Bible. John reported the promise of Jesus, "But the Counselor, the Holy Spirit, whom the Father will send in my name, he will teach you all things, and bring to remembrance all that I have said to you" (14:26).

Dependence on the Spirit who inspired the Scripture is to read the

Bible out of the awareness that God is speaking to us through its sacred pages. This was the firm conviction of the great Reformers in their repeated emphasis on the necessity of "the inner witness of the Holy Spirit."

Calvin was skeptical of the ability or necessity of reason to prove the divinity of Scripture before one could believe it as the Word of God. He believed "that Scripture, carrying its own evidence along with it, deigns not to submit to proofs and arguments, but owes the full conviction with which we ought to receive it to the testimony of the Spirit."[4] He stated further, "For as God alone can properly bear witness to His own words, so these words will not obtain full credit in the hearts of men, until they are sealed by the inward testimony of the Spirit."[5]

The Reformers also laid great stress on what they called the clarity of Scripture. Its great truths were plain enough to be grasped by anyone approaching Scripture in the humility of prayer and faith. Scripture, it was held, is able to authenticate itself and is not dependent on outside external evidences to bolster its truths.

Dependence upon the Spirit for understanding Scripture is an expression of the priesthood of the believer and underscores the necessity of each grasping the truth of Scripture for one's self if faith is to be genuine. However, one must guard against purely subjective, private interpretations that tend to distort the truths of Scripture. Peter reminded us "that no prophecy of Scripture is a matter of one's own interpretation" (2 Pet. 1:20), even as the prophets gave not their own opinions but "moved by the Holy Spirit spoke from God" (v. 21). So we are not to read into Scripture our own pet ideas. With the aid of the Spirit, we are to seek to understand what He inspired the first witnesses to write.

Bible dictionaries, word books, commentaries, the creeds of the early church, the great church confessions, and works of theology are all helpful guides for our own understanding. To check our ideas and interpretations against the best minds of the larger Christian community through the ages keeps us in the main stream of sound biblical interpretation. Knowledge of how the church dealt with various heresies through the centuries helps us avoid the same errors today.

One of the marvels of the Bible is that one does not have to be a scholar to understand its great themes and central truths. However, the Bible puts no premium on ignorance. We are to love God with our minds (Matt. 22:37). God invites us to reason with Him about His great deeds of salvation (Isa. 1:18). The more we learn *about* the Bible the better we can grasp what is *in* the Bible. But there is no substitute for reading the Scriptures, devotionally and prayerfully, out of a humble and seeking faith in the assurance that God keeps His promise to speak to our own individual hearts through its sacred pages. Next to prayer itself, the Bible is our most direct communication with God, and that is never more clearly so than when we make its great prayers our own petitions. The Bible is not to be equated with God, which would be a form of idolatry. We must ever be mindful of its dual nature—it is the Word of God in the words of men, an "earthen vessel, to show that the transcendent power belongs to God and not to us" (2 Cor. 4:7).

The Application to Life

Though written in a language not our own and arising out of a culture vastly different from ours, the Bible, nevertheless, is a most contemporary book. The ultimate task of interpretation, therefore, is to relate its abiding truths to our own needs and situations. One of the marvels is that the Bible can be translated into modern languages without losing its force and power as the Word of God. The message still comes through. That is why the comparison of many translations is such a help to the student of the Bible.

The opening chapters of the Bible (Gen. 1—11) constitute a theological introduction to all of human history. They describe the human situation as we meet it in every age and culture. Our moral and spiritual natures remain the same as does our need of redemption. We stand in the same relationship to God as did Adam: over against our Creator who made us in His image for fellowship with Himself, answerable to God for our stewardship of the earth.

The account of the fall tells us not only how sin began in history but how sin still originates in human experience, bringing alienation from God, making earth no longer an Eden. The judgment in the Flood reminds us that we live in a moral universe in which a moral God allows us to reap what we sow.

But the main thrust of the biblical narrative is to reveal that God is not only the Lord of history and nature but also the Redeemer who has taken the initiative to reconcile us to Himself. It tells us how He worked through a Chosen People until He sent the promised Messiah in the fullness of time. It tells us how the new community of faith, the church, is the arena through which God is continuing to reach us with His message of grace and redemption.

When we have a sense of God's movement in history and of His offer of redemption in Jesus Christ, we best understand the relevance of the Bible for us and our time. In Jesus Christ, God reveals to us the kind of persons He wants us to be. Jesus' life and teachings become the clues by which we are able to discern the abiding moral and spiritual principles throughout Scripture by which we are to live.

While the Bible does not address itself specifically to many of the moral issues we face in our day, it does provide the moral motivation for dealing with them. It places supreme value on human beings as persons made in God's image and for whom Christ has died. Jesus' statement that the sabbath was made for man sets forth the principle that all human institutions should serve the ends of God's purposes. Jesus' description of the last judgment in Matthew 25 reminds us that love for our fellowman is the ultimate measure of our own moral and spiritual condition.

The Goals of Interpretation

Evangelism

One of the main purposes of biblical interpretation is the proclamation of the gospel. The message of salvation must be plainly set forth. Whether the text is taken from the Old or New Testament, evangelistic interpretation proclaims how the Scriptures make plain our need of redemption and how, in Jesus Christ, God offers His grace and mercy. Evangelistic preaching should also make plain what kind of life the redeemed are to live.

Apologetics

Apologetic interpretation has to do with confronting rival faiths and philosophies with the unique claims of the biblical faith. It seeks to answer the criticisms and challenges brought against the Christian faith by unbelievers. It seeks to clarify Christian doctrine and combat heresy. It seeks to "destroy arguments and every proud obstacle to the knowledge of God, and take every thought captive to obey Christ" (2 Cor. 10:5).

Nurture

Growth in grace and knowledge is an essential of the Christian life. The spiritual life of the believer requires constant care and nurture. Interpretation which meets this need will be more of a devotional nature. It seeks to enrich one's personal pilgrimage of faith. Reading in the great devotional classics of the church will be an invaluable aid to the serious student of the Bible as he or she feeds upon the Word of God.

Notes

1. Broadman Commentary, 1, p. 28.
2. Ibid., p. 29.
3. Donald K. McKim, ed., *The Authoritative Word* (Grand Rapids: Wm. B. Eerdmans, 1983); "The Bible," Donald G. Miller, p. 108.
4. John Calvin, *Institutes of the Christian Religion* (Grand Rapids: Wm. B. Eerdmans, 1957), Henry Beveridge, trans., I, VII 5, p. 72.
5. Ibid.

7
The Authority of the Bible

One of the most important elements in a doctrine of Scripture has to do with the authority of the Bible and the claims it makes for itself. The Bible claims to be the authentic and completely trustworthy record of God's revelation of Himself and His eternal purpose for mankind.

Our understanding of biblical authority grows out of our understanding of the nature of Scripture. What kind of book is the Bible (its unique content and themes)? What about inspiration (how it came into existence)? and What is the divine intention in Scripture (how it fulfills the purpose of God)? These are the primary matters having to do with its unique authority.

Through the centuries many claims have been made *for* the Bible. For some people, the Bible is merely great literature, containing many sublime examples of history, law, poetry, parables, and prophetic oratory. For others, it is a collection of high moral principles. For the student of comparative religions, it is the story of the religious history of a special people in their pilgrimage of faith through the centuries (Israel and the Christian church).

For some, it is a book of prophecy, containing the prerecorded history of the human race. For others, it is a source book for all kinds of philosophical and political movements, as witness the movement of Liberation Theology in our own time. For others, it is a unique collection of devotional literature for the nurture of the individual soul.

There is some truth in all these claims, but none of them deals adequately with the unique claims the Bible makes for itself. We must guard against making claims for the Bible which it does not make for itself. We must take into account wherein the Scriptures distinguish between major themes and minor themes, while still affirming the inspiration of both.

We must take seriously the progressive response to the unfolding revelation as God's purpose and will become clearer and clearer. The Mosaic law on the treatment of slaves is no longer binding on us in the light of God's revelation in Jesus Christ. Christ's atoning death fulfilled the meaning and purpose of the Old Testament sacrificial system, for the law was "but a shadow of the good things to come instead of the true form of these realities" (Heb. 10:1).

By establishing a new covenant, Christ does away with the old covenant. "For if that first covenant had been faultless, there would have been no occasion for a second. In speaking of a new covenant he treats the first as obsolete. And what is becoming obsolete and growing old is ready to vanish away" (Heb. 8:7,13).

As Paul reminded us, Christ is the end (fulfillment) of the law (Rom. 10:4). The law served its purpose as a schoolmaster to bring us to Christ (Gal. 3:24). Often the distinction is made between the ceremonial laws of the Old Testament which are no longer binding and the moral teachings of the Old Testament which are still required of us. Yet the ceremonial law remains as an authoritative witness to the moral character of God and the obedience God required of His people at a particular time in the history of Israel.

The New Testament stands on a higher plane than the Old. It is God's final authority of revelation and redemption. It is the fulfillment and completion of the Old Testament. Jesus Christ and His teachings stand above those of the ancient prophets.

The Nature of Authority

A General Definition of Authority

With a wide range of meaning, our word *authority* comes from the Latin, *auctor,* meaning "originator, beginner, creator, source, author." The term *authority* directs our minds, therefore, to the source of the true reality of any matter under consideration.

We speak of an expert in a given field as an "authority" because he possesses true knowledge of his subject matter. If he is the "author, originator, discoverer" of the truths of reality of his subject matter, he is considered an authority of the highest order. The truth of Scrip-

ture, however, is based on the highest authority possible, inasmuch as
its truths were not based on human discovery "because no prophecy
ever came by the impulse of man, but men moved by the Holy Spirit
spoke from God" (2 Pet. 1:21). God is the Creator and Source of all
truth and reality. His authority stands behind and is communicated
through the Scripture.

The Bible makes equally plain that all human discovery of truth is
a form of general revelation since people can only "discover" what
God has already done in the created order. God is behind all truth
however we come to know it.

The concept of authority includes the idea of power. To exercise
authority means the right and power "to command, to enforce laws,
to exact obedience, and to judge." Again the Bible makes plain that
God alone possesses absolute power and authority. The governing
power (authority) of the state comes from the permissive will of God.
For instance, Pilate arrogantly asked Jesus, "Do you not know that
I have power [authority] to release you, and power [authority] to
crucify you?" To this Jesus replied, "You would have no power
[authority] over me unless it had been given you from above" (John
19:1-11). Paul made the same point in Romans 13:1, "Let every
person be subject to the governing authorities. For there is no authority except from God, and those that exist have been instituted by
God." In the Scripture, power and authority are often interchangea-
ble, and both translate the New Testament term, *exousia*.

Jesus, who is the expression of God's power unto salvation, derives
authority from God. So Jesus prayed "Father, the hour has come;
glorify thy Son that the Son may glorify thee, since thou hast given
him power [*exousia*] over all flesh, to give eternal life to all whom
Thou hast given him. And this is eternal life, that they know thee the
only true God, and Jesus Christ whom thou hast sent" (John 17:1-2).

To those who challenged Jesus' authority, He replied, "For as the
Father has life in himself, so he has granted the Son also to have life
in himself, and has given him authority to execute judgment, because
he is the Son of man. I can do nothing on my own authority; as I hear,
I judge; and my judgment is just, because I seek not my own will but
the will of him who sent me" (John 5:26-27,30). In the last resurrection appearance recorded by Matthew, Jesus reminded His disciples,

"All authority in heaven and on earth has been given to me" (Matt. 28:18).

By *authority,* we mean that which provides sufficient grounds for belief and action and by its inner power is able to call forth faith and obedience based on the true knowledge and experience of reality. The ultimate test of authority, therefore, is whether it can make good its claims.

The Biblical Claim to Authority

Our understanding of the Bible's authority is based on our understanding of what kind of book the Bible is. The Bible itself, both directly and indirectly, tells us what kind of book it is. Where the Scripture makes no direct, explicit claims about certain subjects, it is telling us indirectly what it is not. It does not claim, for example, to be a book on science. However, God is able to use the primitive, prescientific views of the biblical writers as "earthen vessels" (2 Cor. 4:7) through which to communicate an abiding authoritative revelation of Himself and His will for us. When the Bible does touch on the sphere of scientific research (the created order including human history), it always emphasizes God as the sovereign Creator and Lord of nature and history and man's responsibility to Him. It provides a theological mandate for scientific research in God's command to Adam to "subdue the earth, and till the garden." More importantly, it provides principles of moral guidance for the God-honoring and man-serving use of all scientific knowledge. But a main purpose of the Bible was not to impart modern scientific information, which neither the biblical writers nor their readers could have understood at the time.

Nor is the Bible a book on sociology, though it has much to say about how people are to treat each other in all the human relationships of life, political and otherwise. Nor is the Bible a book on economics, though, again, it provides moral and spiritual guidance on our responsibility for stewardship of the earth and our personal possessions, as well as our concern for the poor and needy and the dignity of honest labor.

Nor is the Bible a book on the general history of the human race, though it makes crystal clear God's concern for and lordship over all nations. It is not even a detailed, exhaustive history of Israel and the church, nor of the life of Jesus Himself (John 20:30-31; 21:25). It is a highly selective account of the special events, incidents, and encounters in which God was making Himself known as He worked out His purpose of redemption for all the world.

Nor is the Bible a book on psychology, though one of its central themes is about man's true nature as made in the image of God. It has much to say throughout about human nature, concentrating on how our proper relationship to or alienation from God explains so much about the workings of the human mind. While not primarily a book on morals and ethics, the Bible does concentrate a great deal on the absolute moral requirements of God for us in our personal and social lives.

Nor is the Bible a book on religion in general. It is an accurate account of how Israel's religion developed in response to the divine initiative of God's self-revelation. This revelation freed Israel from the idolatrous practices of her neighbors and reached its fulfillment in the Christian religion, thus providing a touchstone for evaluating the truths of all religions.

What kind of book then is the Bible? What is its main subject matter? What kind of claims does it make for itself directly? Simply stated, from cover to cover, it is about God—His character and purpose, what He is up to in the universe and in our lives. The chief emphasis on the divine activity has to do with God's concern for and relationship to human beings, centering in His initiative in seeking our redemption. The main arena of the divine activity is the realm of human history.

Since *authority* means the right to exercise power unto a given purpose, the Bible focuses on God as the Source of all power. It tells us how God has exercised His power (authority) to accomplish His purpose for humanity. The unique authority of the Bible rests on the fact that it is an authentic witness to God's authority in using His power to achieve His eternal purpose.

The authority of the Bible as witness to God's power is seen in three dimensions: theological, historical, and literary.[1] It has theological authority because it reveals God. It makes known the nature, character, and purpose of the one and only, true and living God, Lord of nature and history, and of all peoples.

Turn to me and be saved,
     all the ends of the earth!
     For I am God, and there is no other.
By myself I have sworn.
     from my mouth has gone forth in righteousness
     a word that shall not return:
"To me every knee shall bow,
     every tongue shall swear" (Isa. 45:22-23).

God is the unifying voice behind all Scripture. He speaks through Scripture, giving His own interpretation of His mighty acts of redemption. The Bible always points "beyond the sacred page" to the living God who is, nevertheless, present among His people to save and deliver. "For I am God and not man,/the Holy One in your midst,/ and I will not come to destroy" (Hos. 11:9). "Shout, and sing for joy, O inhabitant of Zion,/for great in your midst is the Holy One of Israel" (Isa. 12:6).

The Bible provides us with the highest concept of God known to the human mind. Its ideas, concepts, and words about God (and the propositions to be drawn therefrom) have the power to draw us into our own meeting with God Himself. The authority of the Bible rests on the claim that it gives an exact and trustworthy account of God's self-revelation. Therefore, the Scripture possesses historical authority because the books of the Bible alone preserve the account of God's action in the historical events of special revelation. No other collection of documents out of the vast literature of Israel and the church could possibly give a more exact account of those events.

The historical authority of the Bible is derived from its witness to God's redemptive action in history. God displayed His power and authority in the action of creation; with His people, Israel; in the life, death, and resurrection of Christ; in Christ's disciples (the church); and in the Scriptures.[2] All five serve to underline the theological unity of the Bible.

The theme of God as Creator runs throughout Scripture. Through the inspired prophets, God reveals Himself as the Creator of the universe and all living things within it, including especially His people Israel. "I am the Lord, your Holy One,/the Creator of Israel, your King" (Isa. 43:15*a*).

Thus says God, the Lord,
  who created the heavens and stretched them out,
  who spread forth the earth and what comes from it,
who gives breath to the people upon it
  and spirit to those who walk in it:
"I am the Lord, I have called you in righteousness,
  I have taken you by the hand and kept you;
I have given you as a covenant to the people,
  a light to the nations,
  to open the eyes that are blind,
to bring out the prisoners from the dungeon,
  from the prison those who sit in darkness.
I am the Lord, that is my name;
  my glory I give to no other,
  nor my praise to graven images" (Isa. 42:5-8).

Creation is not merely a past event. It continues in the present and moves into the future. "Therefore, if any one is in Christ, he is a new creation; the old has passed away, behold, the new has come" (2 Cor. 5:17). "For behold, I create new heavens/and a new earth,/and the former things shall not be remembered/or come to mind" (Isa. 65:17; cf. 2 Pet. 3:13). The final conquest of sin and the completion of redemption is the work of the Creator God as described in Revelation 21—22. It was revealed to Israel that the God who was dealing with them is none other than He who creates and sustains the world. Though forbidden to worship the nature gods of the neighbors among whom Israel settled, the struggle with Baal worship continued for a long time. Through the inspired prophets, Israel was finally led to worship God as the Lord of nature and not nature itself.

Israel was not to dabble in divination and magic, trying to control nature over which God alone reigned as sovereign Lord. "There shall not be found among you any one who burns his son or his daughter as an offering, any one who practices divination, a soothsayer, or an augur, or a sorcerer, or a charmer, or a medium, or a necromancer [a worshiper of the dead]" (Deut. 18:10). The creation account had made it plain that sun, moon, and stars were to mark the seasons (Gen. 1:14; see Ps. 104:19).

In the Old Testament, the greatest display of God's power (authority) was His free choice of Israel to be His people and His deliverance of them from the bondage of Egypt. The sovereign authority of God is seen in His free election of Israel to be the covenant people through whom He sought the redemption of all mankind.

> It was not because you were more in number than any other people that the Lord set his love upon you and chose you, for you were the fewest of all peoples; but it is because the Lord loves you, and is keeping the oath which he swore to your fathers, that the Lord has brought you out with a mighty hand, and redeemed you from the house of bondage, from the hand of Pharaoh king of Egypt (Deut. 7:7-8).

Always linked to the display of God's power in the Exodus, is Israel's sacred mission.

> You have seen what I did to the Egyptians, and how I bore you on eagles' wings and brought you to myself. Now therefore, if you will obey my voice and keep my covenant, you shall be my own possession among all peoples; for all the earth is mine, and you shall be to me a kingdom of priests and a holy nation (Ex. 19:4-6a).

The prophets, as well as the psalmist, constantly reminded Israel of God's mighty power (Deut. 3:24; Josh. 4:23; Isa. 42:5-8; Neh. 1:10; Hag. 2:5; Pss. 77:15; 81:10). Amos made plain that God is the Lord of all history.

> "Are you not like the Ethiopians to me,
>   O people of Israel?! says the Lord.
> "Did I not bring up Israel from the land of Egypt,
>   and the Philistines from Caphtor and the Syrians from Kir?"
> (Amos 9:7).

The Old Testament clearly witnesses to God's authority over all nations and peoples, as Amos called all nations to moral accountability to God (chs. 1—2).

As Lord of history, God is also Lord of the future as He promised Israel the coming Redeemer (Gen. 3:15; Isa. 7:14; 9:6-7; 52:13 to 53:12). The New Testament is the authoritative account of God's fulfillment of that promise. The four Gospels are the supreme authority for God's unique and final revelation of Himself in history. In the life, death, and resurrection of Jesus as the Christ, we have the historical record of the clearest and mightiest display of God's power to reveal and redeem, "for in him the whole fulness of deity dwells bodily" (Col. 2:9).

The claim of Scripture is that God Himself has come to us in Jesus Christ and has endowed Him with His own authority and power. "But when the time had fully come, God sent forth his Son, born of woman, born under the law, to redeem those who were under the law, so that we might receive adoption as sons" (Gal. 4:4-5).

The Scriptures preserve the record of God's good news "which he promised beforehand through his prophets in the holy scriptures, the gospel concerning his Son, who was descended from David according to the flesh and designated Son of God in power according to the Spirit of holiness by his resurrection from the dead, Jesus Christ our Lord" (Rom. 1:2-4). Jesus Christ is God's own authoritative communication of Himself, the historical record of which is now preserved for us in Scripture. Thus Scripture is the continuing authority of God witnessing to His great deeds of redemption on our behalf.

The rest of the New Testament is the authoritative witness of God continuing to exercise His power and authority through the church. Beginning with the apostles, all believers in Jesus Christ are commissioned with the authority and responsibility to witness to God's saving power in Him (Matt. 28:18-20; Acts 1:2). We are promised God's own power to accomplish our mission (Acts 1:4) through the Holy Spirit as Jesus had promised (John 16:13-15).

The church is commissioned with authority to be the guardian of the faith (Jude 3), having been "built upon the foundation of the apostles and prophets, Christ Jesus himself being the cornerstone, in whom the whole structure is joined together and grows into a holy temple in the Lord; in whom you are also built into it for a dwelling place of God in the Spirit" (Eph. 2:20-22).

Empowered by the presence of His own Spirit, the church is the arena through which Christ continues to exercise God's authority (power) to redeem those who surrender to Him as Lord and Savior. "Jesus said to them again, 'Peace be with you. As the Father has sent me, even so send I you.' And when he had said this, he breathed on them, and said to them, 'Receive the Holy Spirit' " (John 20:21-22).

The authority of the church stands under the authority of the Word of God as preserved in the Scriptures. The inspiration and preservation of the Scriptures are themselves two of the "mighty acts" of God in history. The Scriptures possess unique authority as the bedrock historical documents that recount the events and persons through whom God has revealed Himself. Since the special events of revelation have occurred (Israel, Christ, the church), the Scriptures are now the primary means whereby God continues to reveal Himself and speak to us.

Of the five areas of God's historical revelation of Himself, to which the Scriptures bear witness, four continues to be realities in our own history: creation (Ps. 19:1; Rom. 1:20); Christ in the heart of believers (2 Cor. 5:17; Col. 1:27); the church; and the Scriptures themselves. But the Scriptures alone possess unique authority as God's Word through which, by His Spirit, He interprets for us His presence, power (authority), and purpose in the other three. Under the authority of Scripture, as the church faithfully proclaims the good news of God's saving activity in Christ, God continues to reveal Himself and redeem us, to address us, and to call us to repentance.

The authority of the Bible grows out of the authority of Christ. Biblical authority rests on the claim that Scripture presents to us the all-sufficient, authentic, and infallible witness to God's saving activity in Jesus Christ. The basic authority of the Bible, therefore, centers in its message of salvation, that, "In Christ God was reconciling the world to himself" (2 Cor. 5:19). The trustworthiness of its witness is attested further by what the Bible says about itself in three specific ways.

The Bible's claim to be inspired (*2 Tim. 3:16; 2 Pet. 1:20-21*).—The Bible claims that God's own authority stands behind it and is the source of its written witness. The constant refrain of the prophets that God's Word came to them confirms Peter's inspired affirmation that "no prophecy ever came by the impulse of man, but men moved by the Holy Spirit spoke from God" (2 Pet. 1:21). Paul made the same claim for the gospel he preached, "And we also thank God constantly for this, that when you received the word of God which you heard from us, you accepted it not as the word of men but as what it really is, the word of God, which is at work in you believers" (1 Thess. 2:13). Throughout the New Testament, the apostles, like the prophets of old, preached the gospel out of the consciousness that their message was received from God (1 John 1:1,3,5).

The fulfillment of prophecy is another way in which the Bible affirms its divine authority.—God is a God who keeps all His promises. The Old Testament records the directing presence of God in the history of Israel, as He keeps His word spoken through His inspired messengers and prophets. Having chosen Abram, God kept His Word to send the child of promise to barren Sarah. He kept His word to Moses to deliver His people from the bondage of Egypt, and led them through the wilderness to the Promised Land as He had vowed. Without violating Israel's freedom, through the centuries that followed, dealing with a rebellious and stubborn nation, God kept His word of judgment and deliverance as spoken through the prophets.

Not as a sign of weakness but as evidence of His righteousness, God allowed Israel to go into Exile with the promise,

> And the surviving remnant of the house of Judah shall again take root downward, and bear fruit upward; for out of Jerusalem shall go forth a remnant, and out of Mount Zion a band of survivors. The zeal of the Lord of hosts will accomplish this (Isa. 37:31-32).

In the agony of the Exile, Israel cried out, "My way is hid from the Lord,/and my right is disregarded by my God" (Isa. 40:27). Isaiah voiced the promise of God:

> Have you not known? Have you not heard?
> The Lord is the everlasting God,
>   the Creator of the ends of the earth.
> He does not faint or grow weary,
>   his understanding is unsearchable (v. 28).

The prophet assured Israel further of God's faithfulness as the Lord of history, "I am the Lord, that is my name; my glory I give to no other, nor my praise to graven images. Behold, the former things have come to pass, and new things I now declare; before they spring forth I tell you of them" (Isa. 42:8-9). In time God kept His Word, He brought Israel out of Exile.

Throughout history, God guided Israel through the word of His prophets. "I spoke to the prophets; it was I who multiplied visions, and through the prophets gave parables. By a prophet the Lord brought Israel up from Egypt, and by a prophet he was preserved" (Hos. 12:10,13).

> Surely the Lord God does nothing,
>   without revealing his secret

> to his servants the prophets.
> The lion has roared;
>   who will not fear?
> The Lord God has spoken;
>   who can but prophesy? (Amos 3:7-8).

Through Jeremiah, God promised that He would make a new covenant with the house of Israel (Jer. 31:31-34). In time, He promised to pour out His Spirit upon all flesh (Joel 2:28-29). But God's greatest promise was to send the future Redeemer as a descendant of the house of David through whom God would be the shepherd of His people (Ezek. 34:15-16,23-24). Sustained by the hope of God's promise spoken through the prophets, Israel awaited the coming of the Messiah (Isa. 7:14; 9:2-7; 42:1-4).

The New Testament is the authoritative record of how God kept His promise in the coming of Jesus. All the prophecies of the promised Messiah are fulfilled in Him. The fulfillment was greater than could be expected! God, in the person of His eternal Son, Himself came to fulfill the mission of the promised Messiah. In his Gospel, Matthew constantly cited passages from the Old Testament to show how Jesus fulfilled the ancient prophecies. The earliest preaching of the apostles constantly stressed the same point, as described by C. H. Dodd:

> The prophecies are fulfilled, and the new Age is inaugurated
>   by the coming of Christ.
> He was born of the seed of David.
> He died according to the Scriptures, to deliver us out of
>   the present evil age.
> He was buried.
> He rose on the third day according to the Scriptures.
> He is exalted at the right hand of God, as Son of God and
>   Lord of quick and dead.
> He will come again as Judge and Savior of men.[3]

Jesus carried out His ministry in the consciousness that He was fulfilling the purpose and promises of God as written in the Old Testament. "You search the scriptures, because you think that in them you have eternal life; and it is they that bear witness to me. If you believed Moses, you would believe me, for he wrote of me" (John

5:39,46). "Think not that I have come to abolish the law and the prophets; I have come not to abolish them but to fulfil them" (Matt. 5:17). As the risen Lord, Christ interpreted Himself to the two on the road to Emmaus as the fulfillment of the prophets, "And he said to them, 'O foolish men, and slow of heart to believe all that the prophets have spoken! Was it not necessary that the Christ should suffer these things and enter into his glory?' And beginning with Moses and all the prophets, he interpreted to them in all the scriptures the things concerning himself" (Luke 24:25-27).

Later that same day in the upper room Christ appeared to the rest of the disciples.

> Then he said to them, "These are my words which I spoke to you, while I was still with you, that everything written about me in the law of Moses and the prophets and the psalms must be fulfilled." Then he opened their minds to understand the scriptures, and said to them, "Thus it is written, that the Christ should suffer and on the third day rise from the dead" (Luke 24:44-46).

The New Testament is the authoritative record of eyewitnesses who beheld in Jesus the fulfillment of the Old Testament prophecies of God's promise (1 John 1:1-4).

Possessing only the Old Testament as sacred Scripture, the apostles repeatedly cited from it those passages which enabled them to properly interpret Jesus as the promised Messiah. The Gospels faithfully report Jesus' awareness of Himself as the Son of man who "came not to be served but to serve, and to give his life as a ransom for many" (Mark 10:45), as the fulfillment of Isaiah 53:12. They cited Jesus' own interpretation of His death as the sacrifice that established the new covenant promised through Jeremiah, "for this is my blood of the covenant, which is poured out for many for the forgiveness of sins" (Matt. 26:28; also see Mark 14:24; Luke 22:20; 1 Cor. 11:25). The author of Hebrews elaborated on the death of Christ as the once-for-all sacrifice that established the new covenant, "Therefore he is the mediator of a new covenant, so that those who are called may receive the promised eternal inheritance, since a death has occurred which redeems them from the transgressions under the first covenant" (Heb. 9:15).

He further proclaimed Christ as the all-sufficient High Priest after the order of Melchizedek, citing the messianic Psalm 110 (Heb. 7). A major theme of the entire Epistle was to show how Christ's death fulfilled the sacrificial system of the old covenant which was "but a shadow of the good things to come" (Heb. 10:1).

John reported the fivefold promise of Jesus to return to the disciples through God's Holy Spirit (John 14:16-17,26; 15:26; 16:7-11,12-15), echoing the promise made through Ezekiel 11:19 and Joel 2. Peter interpreted the outpouring of the Spirit at Pentecost as the direct fulfillment of Joel (Acts 2:16-21).

In showing how Jesus fulfilled the Old Testament, the apostles underscored the historical continuity running through both Testaments, what God prepared to do and what He accomplished in the coming of Christ. It was the same God at work. God's own authority stands behind both the promises and the fulfillment. The Bible does not present to us abstract speculations *about* God. It faithfully reports "the mighty acts" of God as they actually occurred among His Chosen People in the realities of their historic existence. God's revelation of Himself took place in datable times, among a specific people, and at specific places.

The authority of the Bible is grounded in the realities of history. It does not come to us from an ivory tower as the armchair philosophy of one person. It comes to us out of the agony and ecstasy of a community of faith, stretching over some fifteen hundred years from among whom selected spokesmen were inspired to give us God's own interpretation of what He was doing and why.

The response to God's presence varied from generation to generation. Some passages reveal God more clearly than others, though equally inspired. While each was God's word spoken to a particular people in their particular situation, each contributed to the wholeness of the narrative, reporting God's movement in history toward the miracle of the incarnation.

The Scriptures testify further to their authority as God's written Word by their frequent reference to certain miracles that often accompanied God's revelation of Himself.—In the Old Testament, God's authority as Creator and Lord of nature and history was most often described as the exercise of His power on behalf of His people. The birth of Isaac, the plagues in Egypt, the deliverance at the Red Sea, and Israel's victories in battle are all attributed to God's miracle-working power.

The Old Testament calls special attention to two groups of miracles —those connected with the Exodus from Egypt and those associated with Elijah and Elisha in 1 and 2 Kings.[4] At times the word of the prophet was accompanied by a miracle (Isa. 38:8). The prophets constantly reminded Israel of God's mighty powers, "Ah Lord God! It is thou who hast made the heavens and the earth by thy great power and by thy outstretched arm! Nothing is too hard for thee" (Jer. 32:17).

The greatest miracle of all as the display of God's power and authority was the resurrection of Christ, as "the keystone of the whole biblical revelation, the strongly attested and utterly congruous sign of God's character of power and love."[5] That God's own power was available to Jesus is attested by the eyewitnesses who observed His miracles, even His enemies (Mark 3:22). He steadfastly resisted the temptation to work miracles to seduce people in believing in Him, as His temptation experiences make plain (Matt. 4:5-7; Luke 4:9-12). He refused to work miracles as demanded by the Pharisees (Mark 8:12; Matt. 12:39; Luke 11:29).

Jesus did not want to be accepted as a wonder-worker. Of the three words used in the New Testament of miracles, *dunamis* ("powers, mighty works"), *teras* ("wonders"), and *sēmeion* ("signs"), the last is the most important. His miracles are signs pointing to Him as the Lord's Messiah. John in his Gospel selected seven signs that reveal God's sovereign power (authority) at work in Jesus: Jesus turned the water to wine; He healed the nobleman's son; He healed the lame man; He fed the multitude; He walked on the water; He healed the blind man; and He raised Lazarus.

The miracle-signs wrought by Jesus are the evidence that God's kingdom (power, authority, sovereignty) was being revealed in Him, as Jesus Himself so regarded them. "But if it is by the finger of God that I cast out demons, then the kingdom of God has come upon you" (Luke 11:20; see Matt. 12:28 which reads "by the Spirit of God").

In answer to the question of John the Baptizer, "Are you he who is to come, or shall we look for another [that is, the Messiah]?" Jesus replied, "Go and tell John what you hear and see: the blind receive their sight and the lame walk, lepers are cleansed and the deaf hear, and the dead are raised up, and the poor have good news preached to them" (Matt. 11:3-5), reflecting the prophecies of Isaiah 35:5-6 and 61:1.

Encompassing the miracles of Jesus are two special miracles wrought directly by God Himself—the miraculous conception and the resurrection. Coming at the beginning and the end of Jesus' sojourn on earth, one might say they are the divine quotation marks God placed around the life of Jesus as His supreme Word of revelation and redemption.

As the written Word of God, the Bible witnesses to its own inspiration and trustworthy recording of the fulfillment of prophecy and the miracles that often accompanied God's self-revelation. The Scriptures underscore their chief claim to authority as the infallible witness to the message of salvation, centering in and reaching its climax in the life, death, and resurrection of Jesus Christ.

Authority and the Function of Scripture

The authority of the Bible arises out of the authority of Christ to whom it bears an inerrant witness. Its function is to make Him known as the One in whom God has supremely revealed Himself for our redemption. The Bible reveals God's purpose to "bring many sons to glory" (Heb. 2:10) through Jesus Christ. It was not written to give us general knowledge on all subjects, nor to disclose truths of God discoverable through the unique God-given endowments that set us apart from other living creatures.

The Bible speaks clearly of its own function to make us "wise unto salvation through faith which is in Christ Jesus" (2 Tim. 3:15, KJV). Writing under inspiration, Paul spelled out further the function of Scripture, "All scripture is inspired by God and profitable for teaching, for reproof, for correction, and for training in righteousness, that the man of God may be complete, equipped for every good work" (2 Tim. 3:16-17). The function of the Bible is twofold: to bring us into our own saving encounter through faith in Jesus Christ and to instruct us in holy living, as God requires.

The proclamation of the apostles was twofold: preaching and teaching. The verb *kērussein,* properly speaking, means "to preach, to proclaim" the good news of Christ. The noun *kerygma* is the message of salvation, whose heartbeat is Christ's death as atonement for sin.

In the eyes of unbelievers, the cross is foolishness, "For the word of the cross is folly to those who are perishing, but to us who are being saved it is the power of God" (1 Cor. 1:18).

True preaching, therefore, is the proclamation of Christ as the crucified Savior and risen Lord. The authority of the Bible resides in the fact that it is an all-sufficient, trustworthy, and infallible record of God's saving deed in Jesus Christ.

> For since, in the wisdom of God, the world did not know God through wisdom, it pleased God through the folly of what we preach to save those who believe. For Jews demand signs and Greeks seek wisdom, but we preach Christ crucified, a stumbling block to Jews and folly to Gentiles, but to those who are called, both Jews and Greeks, Christ the power of God and the wisdom of God (1 Cor. 1:21-25).

Teaching (*didaskein*) is instruction in ethical and holy living. It provides guidance for living the redeemed life. It corresponds to Paul's description of the function of Scripture as "profitable for teaching, for reproof, for correction, and for training in righteousness, that the man of God may be complete, equipped for every good work" (2 Tim. 3:16-17). Paul's letters often exhibit this twofold form of apostolic proclamation. In the first part of his letters, he expounded on the content of the gospel, drawing out the full meaning of God's saving activity in Christ. In the latter part, he gave instruction on living the Christian life. Romans is the clearest example of this division from Paul's Epistles. Romans 1—8 is a full exposition of the content of the gospel; Romans 12—16 sets forth how the Christian is to live in obedience to the gospel. All of the letters of Paul contain both "gospel material" and "teaching material."

Throughout the New Testament, one may discern the distinction between the essential content of the *kerygma* and *didaskein*. The twofold distinction is also clearly indicated in the Great Commission given by the risen Lord to the church.

> All authority in heaven and on earth has been given to me. Go therefore and make disciples of all nations, baptizing them in the name of the Father and of the Son and of the Holy Spirit, teaching them to observe all that I have commanded you; and lo, I am with you always, to the close of the age (Matt. 28:18-20).

The first part of the Commission calls for the proclamation of the *kerygma* that souls may be won and saved. The second part is just as important: Those redeemed must be instructed in obedience to all Christ Himself taught. The preaching and teaching are done on the authority of Christ who abides with His church through the Spirit of truth as the power by which both preaching and teaching are carried on (John 16:13-16).

Paul also voiced the awareness that his preaching and teaching were done through the power of the Spirit:

> So also no one comprehends the thoughts of God except the Spirit of God. Now we have received not the spirit of the world, but the Spirit which is from God, that we might understand the gifts bestowed on us by God. And we impart this in words not taught by human wisdom but taught by the Spirit, interpreting spiritual truths to those who possess the Spirit" (1 Cor. 2:11-13).

While acknowledging God's accommodation to human ways of thinking and speaking in Scripture, the early church fathers thought the Bible's authority resided in its errorless and infallible message of salvation. Especially was this true of Origen, Chrysostom, and Augustine.[6] In protest against the authoritarian teachings of the Roman Church, Luther and Calvin stressed the message of salvation in Scripture as its true authority.[7] Both rejected the idea that reason must first prove the inspiration and authority of Scripture before one could come to a saving knowledge of God through Jesus Christ. Both believed that, by the aid of the Holy Spirit, the clear message of salvation proclaimed by Scripture contained within itself its own authority to convince one of its truth and the claims the Bible makes for itself.

The test of any authority is whether it can make good its claim. Authority is only as real as it has power to accomplish its purpose. Authority takes on many forms, depending on the nature of the power it possesses and the aims it seeks to achieve. It may take an external form, as the power of the state to enforce its laws by coercion, fines, or punishment. In a monarchy, the authority and power reside in the king. In a totalitarian state or dictatorship, the power is in the hands of the dictator. In a democracy or republic, the power is derived from the consent of the governed who delegate authority to act on their behalf through elected officials.

The written word operates on a different level of authority. Its power resides in the ideas and concepts employed to describe the truth of its subject matter. The authority of the written word operates on the power of persuasion. It possesses no external power of coercion. Its power is most persuasive when it is known that its author speaks out of firsthand experience with the reality about which he writes. The written word exercises the highest level of authority and power when it is able to lead us into our own personal experience with its subject matter so as to confirm for ourselves the truth it proclaims.

In regard to its subject matter, its authorship, and its function, the Bible is unique. It is a book about God Who has revealed Himself in history through a Chosen People, Israel, and the church, in order to redeem us. It possesses a dual authorship, being both the Word of God and the words of men. It is a composite book, being actually sixty-six smaller books written by many writers over a period of many centuries with the unifying theme that it is the same God encountered throughout. It states its function simply and clearly, "to make thee wise unto salvation . . . in Christ Jesus" and to instruct, guide, reprove, and train us in living that life of holiness and righteousness required by our Creator God.

The Bible's authority resides in its power of persuasion. Its ideas, concepts, themes, and theological propositions possess the power to persuade and convince the *mind* to accept as true what it affirms. It possesses power to move the *heart* to adoration, wonder, and praise. It possesses the power to motivate the *will* to obedience.

It possesses no power of external coercion. It is overwhelming in its persuasion that its writers spoke and wrote out of firsthand encounter with the God of creation. The Bible's highest level of power and authority is confirmed by the fact that obedience to its claims and guidance does actually lead us into our own experience of saving faith.

It exercises its authority in the same way Jesus exercised His authority: not by coercion but by persuasion, by facing us with the facts of God's dealings with Israel; the life, death, and resurrection of Jesus Christ; and the changed lives of the disciples who confessed Jesus as the Savior. It invites us to the same pilgrimage of faith. It says to us, "Come see for yourself!"

The Bible confronts us with the awesome fact that God never forces Himself on us. Approached with an open mind, a prayerful heart, earnestly seeking to know the truth of God, the Bible convinces us by its own inner power that "the word of God is living and active, sharper than any two-edged sword, piercing to the division of soul and spirit, of joints and marrow, and discerning the thoughts and intensions of the heart" (Heb. 4:12).

From within its own pages, the Bible affirms its authority as the trustworthy record of God's self-revelation and of His offer of salvation through Jesus Christ. The changed lives of the disciples, who confessed Christ as Messiah and Savior, are clear evidence that it makes good its claims in fulfilling its function as the power of God unto salvation. The changed lives of multitudes through the centuries is further evidence that the claims of Scripture can be verified in human experience.

The Authority of Christian Doctrine

Through the centuries, the church has set forth the teaching of Scripture in the form of doctrinal statements. The earliest form of such statements was expressed in certain "rules of faith" and the Apostles' Creed as baptismal confessions of faith. In order to standardize the pure doctrine of the church in its struggle with heresy, there sprang from the rule of faith the ancient creeds of the early church councils.[8]

The effort was to reach a consensus on the official doctrine of the church as to what was believed everywhere, always and by all. By the time of the Reformation, the church had assumed an authoritarian position with power to impose its doctrinal teachings on all true believers. It had also developed many doctrines hard to substantiate from the Scriptures. At that point, Luther and the other Reformers sought to bring the authority of the church and all its teachings under the principle of *sola scriptura*—the supreme authority of the Scriptures.

Following the Reformation, many confessions of faith were written, setting forth the orthodox and official doctrinal position of the various branches of Protestantism. Each in its own way dealt with the authority of Scripture as a major doctrine of the faith with special emphasis on "the Bible to be interpreted in the light of its witness to God's work of reconciliation in Christ."[9]

The authority of councils, creeds, and confessions versus the authority of Scripture continues to be a lively issue among all Christian bodies. For some, authority still resides in the power of the church to impose its creedal statements upon its adherents. Resistance to creedalism is a major characteristic of the churches which seek to adhere more closely to the Reformation principles of (1) justification by faith in Jesus Christ alone; (2) the supreme authority of Scripture for faith and practice; and (3) the priesthood of the believer with its emphasis on the freedom of the individual, under the guidance of the Holy Spirit, to interpret Scripture for oneself.

Nevertheless, one is not to discount the value for understanding Scripture to be gained by the guidance afforded by prayerful study of the great confessions and doctrinal statements of the various churches, including the classical theological works at our disposal.

The basic question we face here is the nature of authority for belief. Is belief to be imposed from without, or can the Scriptures be trusted, as the Word of God, to speak directly to our own hearts? The deeper question has to do with the nature of genuine faith: Is it to be imposed from without, or is it one's own free response to the hearing of the gospel?

Nowhere does the Bible say we are saved by believing doctrine— merely giving intellectual assent to ideas *about* God and Jesus Christ. The Bible directs us to faith as personal trust in Jesus as Savior and Lord. Faith comes by hearing the *kerygma*—the preaching of the gospel. "So faith comes from what is heard, and what is heard comes by the preaching of Christ" (Rom. 10:17).

Calvin described faith as "a firm and sure knowledge of the divine favour toward us, founded on the truth of a free promise in Christ, and revealed to our minds, and sealed on our hearts, by the Holy Spirit."[10] The authority of Scripture resides in its power to engender such faith. Its authority stands above all other written authorities. Doctrinal statements have authority as faithful guides only as they are true to Scripture.

The Bible as the Word of God

No writer of any biblical book made reference to the whole Bible as we now know it. The concept of the Bible as a single book was not possible until after AD 367. At that time, the twenty-seven books of the New Testament were added to the thirty-nine books of the Old

Testament to form a single volume of sacred writings considered by Christians as the authentic record of God's self-revelation of Himself in history.

Because God is the inspiring Author of each of the books, we can use the term "the Word of God" in a collective sense in speaking of the Bible as a whole. God is the One speaking throughout its sacred pages. When different books of the Bible use the phrase "the word of God," they do so in a variety of ways. The concept of "the word of God" is a basic category for understanding how God communicates with us, drawing on the wonder and mystery of language and speech as the most meaningful way in which one mind communicates with another mind.

In the Bible, therefore, the phrase "the word of God" became the essential means whereby God revealed Himself and His purposes. One of the miraculous wonders of the Bible is how God could use the ordinary language of earth through which to communicate His eternal Word. We must always remember that the Bible is the Word of God in the earthen vessels of the words of men "to show that the transcendent power belongs to God and not to us," as Paul reminded us (2 Cor. 4:7). God used the words already known to the inspired writers through which to reveal Himself and His purposes.

It is important to know something of the meaning of the term for *word* as used by the biblical writers. The basic term for *word* in the Old Testament is *dabar* (pronounced davar) with a rich variety of meanings: it can mean spoken utterance, a saying, speech, narrative, command, message, request, promise; it can also mean a thing, an affair, an event.[11]

The basic term in the New Testament is *logos*. Thayer cites three special usages of it in the New Testament: (1) it can mean speech, language, words, discourse, narrative, declared thought, instruction, teaching, doctrine, report of a deed or event, decree, order, mandate, or message;[12] (2) logos can also mean the content of the mind as reason, ideas, concepts, cause, ground of reality, thought;[13] and (3) its special use in John's Gospel as a description of Christ as the incarnate Word of God in which God's reason and power of creation and redemption are most perfectly disclosed in Him.[14]

The phrase "the Word of God" is used in the Scriptures more often in a collective sense to refer to the totality of God's communication in all the rich variety of ways in which He speaks to us through the prophets and the apostles. Nowhere does the Bible equate itself with God Himself. Because it is His Word of revelation and redemption, the Bible is to be revered and honored but never deified. We must always be on our guard against bibliolatry. The Bible always points beyond itself to the living God. As the written Word of God, its supreme witness is to Christ as the living Word through whom God has perfectly revealed Himself and speaks to us most clearly.

As the living Word, Jesus Christ is the grand summary and climax of God's revealing Word, as the author of Hebrews reminds us:

> In many and various ways God spoke of old to our fathers by the prophets; but in these last days he has spoken to us by a Son, whom he appointed the heir of all things, through whom also he created the world. He reflects the glory of God and bears the very stamp of his nature, upholding the universe by his word of power (Heb. 1:1-3).

The Authority of Jesus Christ as the Living Word of God

The idea of authority contains within its meaning the concept of power. Authority is the power "to command, to act, to achieve a given purpose." As the Creator, Source of all reality and power, God is the supreme Authority who exercises His power over all the works of His hands. All earthly authorities and powers are derived from Him, as the Scriptures make plain (Rom. 13:1).

God authorized the inspired writers of the Bible to be His spokesmen through whom He interpreted the display of His power in creation, revelation, and redemption. They spoke with authority God's Word as given to them. He authorized the prophets of old to proclaim the promise of the coming Redeemer. But the supreme exercise of God's authority and power was displayed in the life, death, and resurrection of Jesus Christ.

The Miracle of the Incarnation

In the Old Testament, the word of God and the prophet were two separate entities, as they witnessed to the events of revelation. In Jesus Christ, the divine Word and Deed are one and the same event. In Him the eternal Logos (God's power, reason, and purpose by which He created all things) became flesh in the man Jesus, as the opening verses of John's Gospel declare:

> In the beginning was the Word, and the Word was with God, and the Word was God. He was in the beginning with God; all things were made through him, and without him was not anything made that was made. In him was life, and the life was the light of men. And the Word became flesh and dwelt among us, full of grace and truth; we have beheld his glory, glory as of the only Son from the Father. For the law was given through Moses; grace and truth came through Jesus Christ. No one has ever seen God; the only Son, who is in the bosom of the Father, he has made him known" (John 1:1-4,14,17-18).

The consistent witness and claim of the New Testament is that God Himself is present in Jesus, exercising His authority and power. As the "Word made flesh," Christ is God's declaration of Himself in terms most easily grasped by us, namely the real humanity of Jesus. "He reflects the glory of God and bears the very stamp of his nature" (Heb. 1:3).

The Old Testament had already revealed that by His Spirit God accomplished His purposes. His Spirit brooded over the chaos of waters at creation's dawn (Gen. 1:2). By His Spirit, He endowed mankind with that power of life which makes us unique as creatures made in His image (Gen. 1:27; 2:7). By His Spirit, He sustains all living creatures (Ps. 104:30) and endows man with special skills (Ex. 31:3-6). By His Spirit, God is present throughout the created order from which no one can flee (Ps. 139:7).

The most important activity of God's Spirit in the Old Testament was when He spoke through the prophets (1 Sam. 19:20; 2 Sam. 23:2; Isa. 61:1; Ezek. 2:2; Mic. 3:8). Through the prophets, God promised the outpouring of His Spirit in the future day of redemption (Isa. 42:1; 44:3; Ezek. 18:31; 36:26-27; Joel 2:28 *ff.*).

Through the power and authority of His Spirit, God accomplishes His saving purpose through Jesus Christ, beginning with the miraculous conception. At Jesus' baptism, the Spirit descended upon Him to remain throughout His lifetime as the source of His power (John 1:33), "For he whom God has sent utters the words of God, for it is not by measure that he gives the Spirit; the Father loves the Son, and has given all things into his hand" (John 3:34-35). Coming up out of the baptismal waters, a voice from heaven said to Jesus, "Thou art my beloved Son; with Thee I am well pleased" (Luke 3:22), calling to mind reference in Psalm 2 to the Messiah and Isaiah 42 which promised the Spirit to be poured out on God's servant.

Led by the Spirit into the wilderness, Jesus won His battle against the Evil One after which He returned in the power of the Spirit to begin His Messianic mission (Luke 4:1-14). Henceforth, the entire life of Jesus was a manifestation of the power of God's Spirit working through Him (Matt. 12:28).

John's Gospel draws out the full meaning of the miracle of the incarnation—that Jesus is both human and divine. John repeatedly testified of Jesus as the One whom God has sent, His origin and abode are with the Father in eternity (John 3:17,28; 4:34; 5:23-24,30,38; 6:29-44; 7:28-29).

Jesus fulfilled His mission out of the awareness that He spoke and acted with God's own authority. "I can do nothing on my own authority; as I hear, I judge; and my judgment is just, because I seek not my own will but the will of him who sent me" (John 5:30). He spoke with an authority greater than that of Moses and the prophets in the oft-repeated formula, "You have heard it said. . . . But I say to you" (Matt. 5:21-22).

He attached a finality to His words that became God's own offer of eternal life, "Truly, truly, I say to you, he who hears my word and believes him who sent me, has eternal life; he does not come into judgment, but has passed from death to life" (John 5:24). Jesus spoke with the final authority of God Himself, "My teaching is not mine, but his who sent me; if any man's will is to do his will, he shall know whether the teaching is from God or whether I am speaking on my own authority" (John 7:16-17).

Jesus' whole life—his teachings, deeds, and supremely His death—are God's living Word spoken to us. Jesus Himself became the gospel preached by the apostles. He is the message of salvation. One's eternal salvation rides on the acceptance of His words, "For whoever is ashamed of me and my words, of him will the Son of man be ashamed when he comes in his glory and the glory of the Father and of the holy angels (Luke 9:26). In speaking of Himself as the Bread of Life, Jesus made it plain that we take Him into our lives by feeding on His words, "As the living Father sent me, and I live because of the Father, so he who eats me will live because of me. It is the spirit that gives life, the flesh is of no avail; the words that I have spoken to you are spirit and life" (John 6:57,63). His words are to be planted in our hearts as the seed of the kingdom (Mark 4:1-20; Matt. 13:18-23; Luke 8:4-15).

In the rest of the New Testament, the phrase "the word of God" most often refers to the gospel as the message of God's salvation in Jesus Christ (Acts 11:1; 13:26,46; 18:11; Phil. 2:16; Col. 3:16; 2 Thess. 3:1; 2 Tim. 2:9; Titus 2:5). The essential content of the message is Jesus Christ as the eternal Son of God, the Savior and Messiah. Peter made it clear that the new birth comes through the power of this word, "You have been born anew, not of perishable seed but of imperishable, through the living and abiding word of God" (1 Pet. 1:23).

Citing the promise of God in Isaiah 40:8 that His word is to abide forever, Peter applied the prophecy to the gospel, "Those who preached the good news [the gospel] to you through the Holy Spirit sent from heaven" (1 Pet. 1:12; also see v. 25), even as Jesus had claimed earlier, "Heaven and earth will pass away, but my words will not pass away" (Matt. 24:35; Luke 21:33). He is God's living Word that abides forever.

How does Christ abide still as God's living Word? Through the resurrection. Through the mightiest display of His power in the resurrection, God confirmed the authority which Jesus had exercised during His earthly ministry on God's behalf. Though the revelation of Himself in Jesus Christ was complete and final, God's work of redemption is not yet finished. The same Spirit of God by which the eternal Logos (Word) was made flesh in Jesus is now at work in the church to make Him known to all the world. In making Jesus known, God is made known. So the apostle clearly expressed the mind of Christ, "He who has seen me has seen the Father" (John 14:9).

When Jesus sent forth His disciples with the gospel message, "The kingdom of heaven is at hand" (Matt. 10:7), He assured them that they need not be overanxious about what to say, "for it is not you who speak, but the Spirit of your Father speaking through you" (v. 20). Again John's Gospel brings out the full meaning of Jesus' promise in the five sayings on the coming of the Holy Spirit which He and the Father would send. As the Spirit of truth, His function is to interpret

Christ. Through the Spirit, Christ will continue to lead and instruct His disciples.

> I have yet many things to say to you, but you cannot bear them now. When the Spirit of truth comes, he will guide you into all the truth; for he will not speak on his own authority, but whatever he hears he will speak, and he will declare to you the things that are to come. He will glorify me, for he will take what is mine and declare it to you (John 16:12-14).

The promise includes the assurance that Christ through God's Spirit will abide with us. "All that the Father has is mine; therefore I said that he will take what is mine and declare it to you. A little while, and you will see me no more; again a little while, and you will see me. I came from the Father and have come into the world; again, I am leaving the world and going to the Father" (John 16:15-16,28).

In His high priestly prayer, Christ petitioned the Father that the disciples may share in the oneness He and the Father enjoy, "I in them and thou in me, that they may become perfectly one, so that the world may know that thou hast sent me and hast loved them even as thou hast loved me" (John 17:23).

As the risen Lord, Christ commissioned the disciples to carry on His own saving mission through the power of the Spirit. "Jesus said to them again, 'Peace be with you. As the Father has sent me, even so I send you.' And when he had said this, he breathed on them and said to them, 'Receive the Holy Spirit' " (John 20:21-22).

At Pentecost, the Spirit was poured out on the church as a whole, fulfilling the promise made through Joel. While the appearances of the risen Christ ceased in the New Testament, the awareness of His presence has not ceased to this day. The rest of the New Testament makes plain that the Spirit of God and the Spirit of Christ are the same (Rom. 8:9,11). Through the preaching of the gospel—"the gospel of the glory of Christ, who is the likeness of God" (2 Cor. 4:4)—salvation comes to all who will hear and believe.

> Now the Lord is the Spirit, and where the Spirit of the Lord is, there is freedom. And we all, with unveiled face, beholding the glory of the Lord, are being changed into his likeness from one degree of glory to another; for this comes from the Lord who is the Spirit (2 Cor. 3:17-18).

In the Scriptures, the term "glory" always refers to those times and ways in which God has revealed Himself. The New Testament witnesses to the life of Jesus Christ as the one through whom God has manifested His greatest glory. As the Old Testament constantly refers to God as the Creator who is making Himself known in Israel, so the New Testament makes us aware also that it is the Creator who has made Himself known in Jesus Christ. "For it is the God who said, 'Let light shine out of darkness [Gen. 1:6],' who has shone in our hearts to give the light of the knowledge of the glory of God in the face of Christ" (2 Cor. 4:6).

Christ is the living Word of God, first incarnate in Jesus as "the word made flesh," now made known through the preaching of the gospel "through the Holy Spirit sent from heaven" (1 Pet. 1:12). Though we have this treasure in earthen vessels, the words of men in the Scripture as Paul reminded us (2 Cor. 4:7), the transcendent power belongs to God. As the gospel is preached (all that God has said and done in Jesus Christ), one is made aware that "In Christ God was reconciling the world to himself" (2 Cor. 5:19). And to all who believe, He gives power to become the children of God (John 1:12).

That the Bible speaks with God's own authority about these matters is confirmed in the saving experience of untold multitudes who have found God, and been found by Him, in the preaching of the good news about how God has come to us in Jesus Christ.

Christ as Center of Faith

As the function of Scripture is "to make us wise unto salvation in Jesus Christ," the Scriptures make plain that He is the center of saving faith. The Bible leads us into our own personal encounter with Him. It is the authoritative record of God's revelation of Himself in Israel, Jesus Christ, and the church. The Bible alone contains the full content of the gospel which "is the power of God for salvation to everyone who has faith, to the Jew first and also to the Greek. For in it the righteousness of God is revealed through faith for faith; as it is written, 'He who through faith is righteous shall live' " (Rom. 1:16-17).

"For man believes with his heart and so is justified, and he confesses with his lips and so is saved. So faith comes from what is heard, and what is heard comes by the preaching of Christ" (Rom. 10:10,17). "Through him you have confidence in God, who raised him from the dead and gave him glory, so that your faith and hope are in God. Without having seen him you love him; though you do not now see him you believe in him and rejoice with unutterable and exalted joy. As the outcome of your faith you obtain the salvation of your souls" (1 Pet. 1:21,8-9).

Faith in Christ first of all means our personal trust in Him as Savior—accepting God's free gift of mercy and forgiveness out of His infinite grace (Eph. 2:8). Faith also means obedience to Him as Lord, "for we are his workmanship, created in Christ Jesus for good works, which God prepared beforehand, that we should walk in them" (Eph. 2:10). Therefore the function of the Bible is both *kerygma* (preaching the gospel) and *didaskein* (teaching), guiding us in the life of obedience to God's will. It is a lamp to our feet and a light to our path (Ps. 119:105). It is the all-sufficient and infallible Word of God for faith and practice. Christ is the key and clue by which it is to be interpreted for God uses it to form Christ within us as our hope of glory (Col. 1:27).

"Beyond the Sacred Page"

The Bible seldom calls attention to itself. When it does, it is for the purpose of assuring us that it comes from God. It never presents itself to be the object of faith. It always points beyond itself to the living God. It directs us to put our faith in the living God who has made Himself known in His mighty deeds of revelation and redemption which reached its climax and fulfillment in the life, death, and resurrection of Jesus Christ. It is an inerrant witness to that revelation.

"The Bible is authoritative because it points beyond itself to the absolute authority, the living and transcendent Word of God."[15] The authority and infallibility of the Bible have their basis in Christ and His gospel. The glory of its power is that the Word of God is communicated through its words. Calvin said, "We must remember, that there is an inseparable relation between faith and the word, and that these can no more be disconnected from each other than rays of light from the sun. . . . It is always by his word that he manifests himself to those whom he designs to draw to himself."[16]

As God's witness to Himself, always pointing beyond itself to Him, the Bible is the means by which God continues to address us. To all who open its sacred pages and listen with prayerful, seeking hearts, God speaks. All who accept its message of salvation and put their trust in Christ the living Word enter into the joy of God's eternal kingdom.

On June 2, 1953, Elizabeth II was crowned queen of England. She wore on her head the crown of Saint George encrusted with three thousand diamonds. She wore a gown embroidered with the emblem of the Commonwealth, outlined in gold, silver, and pearls. She held in her hand a globe of the world studded with precious jewels and a silver scepter, symbol of her power as ruling monarch. At a certain time in the ceremony, she was approached by the Queen's chaplain from Scotland who placed in her hands a small book, bound in black leather. He did not place in her hands a copy of Plato's *Republic* nor Augustine's *City of God* nor Thomas More's *Utopia* nor Adam Smith's *Wealth of Nations* nor King John's *Magna Charta.* He placed in her hands a copy of the Bible and said, "Herein is wisdom, earth's greatest treasure. Here is the Royal Law, here are the lively oracles of God!"

One of God's gifts of grace to us is the Bible. We can hold in our own hands "God's lively oracles." Through it God speaks to our own hearts and needs. Through it God offers His great salvation in Christ to all who will accept it for what it says it is—the Word of God in truth!

It is to be properly honored and revered, as the following anonymous tribute makes plain.

The Bible

This BOOK contains—The mind of God, the state of man, the way of Salvation, the doom of Sinners, and the happiness of Believers. Its doctrines are holy, its precepts binding, its histories are true, and its decisions are immutable. Read it to be wise, believe it to be safe and practice it to be holy. It contains light to direct you, food to support you and comfort to cheer you. It is the traveler's map, the pilgrim's staff, the pilot's compass, the soldier's sword, and the Christian's charter. Here Paradise is restored, Heaven opened, and the gates of Hell disclosed. CHRIST IS ITS GRAND SUBJECT, our good its design, and the glory of God its end. It should fill the memory, rule the heart and guide the feet. Read it slowly, frequently, prayerfully. It is a mine of wealth, a paradise of glory, and a river of pleasure. It is given you in life, will be opened at the judgment, and be remembered forever. It involves the highest responsibility, will reward the greatest labor, and condemn all who trifle with its sacred contents.

All because beyond the sacred page God makes *Himself* known!

Notes

1. A. Berkeley Mickelsen, *Interpreting the Bible* (Grand Rapids: Wm. B. Eerdmans, 1974), p. 86.

2. Ibid., pp. 86-95.

3. C. H. Dodd, *The Apostolic Preaching and Its Developments* (Edinburgh: R & R Clark, Ltd., 1949), p. 17.

4. Alan Richardson, *A Theological Word Book of the Bible* (New York: The Macmillan Co., 1951), p. 152.

5. Ibid., p. 153.

6. Jack B. Rogers and Donald K. McKim, *The Authority and Interpretation of the Bible* (San Francisco: Harper and Row, 1979), pp. 11-27.

7. Ibid., pp. 78-88, 97-107.

8. J. L. Neve, *A History of Christian Thought* (Philadelphia: The Muhlenberg Press, 1946). pp. 136, 173.

9. McKim and Rogers, p. 471.

10. John Calvin, *Institutes of the Christian Religion* (Grand Rapids: Wm. B. Eerdmans, 1957), Henry Beveridge, trans., III 11 7, p. 375.

11. Richardson, pp. 283-285.

12. Joseph H. Thayer, *A Greek-English Lexicon of the New Testament* (New York: Harper and Brothers, 1889), pp. 380-382.

13. Ibid.

14. Ibid.

15. McKim, *The Authoritative Word,* "The Primacy of Scripture," Donald G. Bloesch, p. 132.

16. Calvin, III ii 6, pp. 473, 474.

8
Revelation and Redemption

How can we know God? The Bible makes the unique claim that we can know God because God has made a special revelation of Himself, the record of which is contained in Scripture. Knowledge of God is possible because we have been endowed with God-given capacities to know our Creator. We have "response-ability"; we are answerable to Him who is constantly addressing us. Scripture also makes plain the purpose of God's revelation—to reclaim a lost humanity, to redeem us, to reconcile us to Himself, to restore His image in us, to prepare us for His eternal kingdom. Scripture makes known to us God's eternal purposes.

The Divine Intention

In Creation

The first "mighty act of God" recorded in Scripture is the revealed account of creation which is the framework needed to understand the unfolding drama of revelation as narrated in the rest of the Bible. In the course of her history, Israel was made aware that the God dealing with her as Lord and Redeemer is none other than the Almighty God of Creation Himself (Isa. 40:28; 42:5-9; 43:3,14-15), who alone is God (Isa. 44:6).

The creation account sets forth the basic world view of the Bible. Out of His infinite wisdom and power, God has freely chosen to create the world (Ps. 104:24) upon whom all living creatures are dependent (Ps. 104:27-30). Our scientific knowledge of the world confirms the testimony of the prophet that "he did not create it a chaos,/he formed it to be inhabited!" (Isa. 45:18). The creation account stresses the fact

157

that God's chief concern is for human beings—the creature made in His image (Gen. 1:27; 5:1-2) as the crown of His creation.

Man is made for *communion* with his Maker. Our true life is to be one of fellowship with God, in a right relationship of loving trust and faithful obedience. Man is made for *companionship,* for "it is not good that man should be alone" (Gen. 2:18). To be a person is to be in right relationship to other persons. Man is made for *conquest,* appointed by God to exercise "dominion" over the earth, to "subdue it" (Gen. 1:28) and "till the garden" (Gen. 1:26-27; 2:15; Ps. 8:5-8). We are not owners for "the earth is the Lord's and the fulness thereof" (Ps. 24:1); we are God's tenants and stewards.

The created order is God's first and continuing Word to us about His purpose (Ps. 19:1-4; Rom. 1:20). As general revelation, it still speaks to the heart of human beings everywhere, as the Sioux Indians once chanted, "All over the sky a sacred voice is calling."[1] And as the poet testifies to man's prayerful and keen observation of nature,

> He seems to hear a Heavenly Friend,
> And thro' thick veils to apprehend
> A labor working to an end.[2]

But God's Word in Scripture interprets for us God's intention in creation as God's "mighty work" through which He purposes to bring "many sons to glory" through Jesus Christ (Heb. 2:10).

In Redemption

The most important activity of God recorded in Scripture is His "mighty works" to redeem a lost and estranged humanity. The opening chapters of Genesis set forth clearly the cause and plight of our sinful nature—the Adamic rebellion which engulfs us all (Gen. 3) and the banishment from Eden as symbol of our estrangement and the broken relationships of life. The accounts of Noah and the Flood (Gen. 6—9) and the tower of Babel (Gen. 11) disclose history as a moral arena in which a righteous God brings judgment on a rebellious and fallen race.

But God did not give up on mankind nor forsake His purpose in Creation. Through His covenant with Abram, He promised to bless "all the families of the earth" (Gen. 12:3).

Following God's mighty deliverance of His people from the bondage of Egypt, He constituted Israel as a nation bound to Him in covenant love to be "a kingdom of priests and a holy nation" (Ex. 19:4-6). Through punishment and deliverance, in all the long years of Israel's rebellious history, by the Word given to His prophets, God sought to keep Israel true to her mission to be "a light to the nations" (Isa. 42:6). God's concern was to reach all mankind through Israel, "turn to me and be saved,/all the ends of the earth!/For I am God, and there is no other" (Isa. 45:22). God's intention was to provide salvation for all peoples everywhere. He is mightily at work to reconcile the world to Himself, to restore us to our right relationship to Himself, to others, to the world, and to ourselves.

Through the promised remnant (Isa. 10:20-23), God moved forward in history to keep His greatest promise for all—to send the Messiah-Redeemer (Isa. 9:6-7; 52:13 to 53:12). God Himself came in the person of His eternal Son. "No one has ever seen God; the only Son, who is in the bosom of the Father, he has made him known" (John 1:18). "For in him the whole fulness of deity dwells bodily. He reflects the glory of God and bears the very stamp of his nature: (Col. 2:9; Heb. 1:3).

In Jesus Christ, God made the final and complete revelation of Himself: "He who has seen me has seen the Father" (John 14:9). In Him, God completed His work of redemption through His wisdom and power in the cross (1 Cor. 1:18-25) and the glory of the resurrection (Rom. 1:1-6). In Him the Way, the Truth, and the Life of salvation are provided for all.

In Scripture

The authentic and authoritative record of God's mighty acts of revelation and redemption is preserved for us in the books of the Bible. Apart from the Bible, we would not know of God's special deeds of revelation and redemption in Israel, Jesus Christ, and the church. The Bible was not a book dropped down from heaven as a single volume. It recounts faithfully the actual events in history out of which it arose. It is God's own interpretation of Himself through the inspired writers chosen by Him to preserve the record of His revelation. As such, therefore, it speaks with God's own authority.

The Bible always points beyond itself to the living God and the historical events in which He has made Himself known. Its central witness is to Jesus Christ as the living Word of God. The word by which God spoke the world into existence (Gen. 1:3-25; John 1:1-3; 2 Pet. 3:5) became flesh in Him (John 1:14).

As an indispensable and infallible witness to Jesus Christ, God's Spirit now uses Scripture "to make [us] wise unto salvation" in Him. God's intention in Scripture was not only to preserve an accurate record of His revealing and redemptive acts but also to guide us into our own saving encounter with Him. In the Bible, God has provided a lamp unto our feet and a light to our path as we live the life of holy obedience required of us.

The Way of Salvation

By Proclamation of the Living Word

We come to know Christ as Savior by hearing the gospel preached. "For man believes with his heart and so is justified, and he confesses with his lips and so is saved. So faith comes from what is heard, and what is heard comes by the preaching of Christ" (Rom. 10:10,17).

Preaching aims at bringing the hearer into an encounter with Christ Himself. Preaching is another form of God's word when it is true to the Scriptures, God's written Word. In the proclamation of the gospel, Christ is re-presented to the world.

Through preaching the gospel (the *kerygma*—the life, death, and resurrection of Jesus Christ), the salvation God has provided in Christ is offered to all who will receive it. In preaching, God Himself addresses us. "So we are ambassadors for Christ, God making His appeal through us" (2 Cor. 5:20; see 1 Thess. 2:13; John 16:12-15; Matt. 28:18-20).

By New Birth Through the Spirit

Salvation is the gift of new life in Christ through the power of the Holy Spirit. It is like being born all over again (John 3:3-6). "For as the Father has life in himself, so he has granted the Son also to have life in himself" (John 5:26). "I came that they may have life, and have it abundantly" (John 10:10).

Though dead in trespasses and sins (Eph. 2:1), Christ, who is the Resurrection and the Life (John 11:25), raises us to new life in Him.

"For the law of the Spirit of life in Christ Jesus has set me free from the law of sin and death" (Rom. 8:2).

Salvation is dying to self and being raised to new life in Christ, symbolized in the burial waters of baptism, "so that as Christ was raised from the dead by the glory of the Father, we too might walk in newness of life" (Rom. 6:4). "If the Spirit of him who raised Jesus from the dead dwells in you, he who raised Christ Jesus from the dead will give life to your mortal bodies also through his Spirit which dwells in you" (Rom. 8:11). Christ as the new Adam is a life giving Spirit (1 Cor. 15:45). The redeemed life is life lived in and by the Spirit of God, who is also the Spirit of Christ (2 Cor. 3:17).

By Restoration of the Divine Image

God's original purpose in creation to bring "many sons to glory" (Heb. 2:10) is fulfilled in Christ as the redeemed are "conformed to the image of his Son" (Rom. 8:29). Christ is not only the revelation of God but also the revelation of the kind of person we were intended to be. As "the image of the invisible God, the first-born of all creation" (Col. 1:15), bearing "the very stamp of his nature" (Heb. 1:3) in whom "the fulness of God was pleased to dwell" (Col. 1:19), we see in Christ the God in whose image man was first created (Gen. 1:27; 5:1-2).

Salvation is putting on "the new nature, which is being renewed in knowledge after the image of its creator" (Col. 3:10). Beholding the glory of God in the face of Jesus Christ, we are "changed into his likeness from one degree of glory to another; for this comes from the Lord who is the Spirit" (2 Cor. 3:18; see 4:6). "Just as we have borne the image of the man of dust, we shall also bear the image of the man of heaven" (1 Cor. 15:49).

By Fellowship in the Covenant Community

While salvation is personal, it is never a purely private matter. God's revealing and redemptive acts occur in and through a community of faith bound to Him by His ordained covenants of grace, first in Israel and finally in the church. Spiritually speaking, to be a Christian is to be a member of the church, God's new covenant community. Discipleship and churchmanship are two sides of the same coin.

Being born again by the Spirit makes us members of God's spiritual family who "destined us in love to be his sons through Jesus Christ, according to the purpose of his will" (Eph. 1:5; see John 1:12). As "members of the household of God" (Eph. 2:19), we become irrevocably brothers and sisters to all others in God's family.

Replacing the Temple on Mount Zion, the church becomes God's new spiritual temple in which believers "like living stones" are "built into a spiritual house, to be a holy priesthood, to offer spiritual sacrifices acceptable to God through Jesus Christ" (1 Pet. 2:5). Built upon the foundation of the apostles and prophets (as known in Scripture), as the chief cornerstone, Christ is the one "in whom the whole structure is joined together and grows into a holy temple in the Lord; in whom you also are built into it for a dwelling place of God in the Spirit" (Eph. 2:21-22).

Christ not only died for us one by one but also for the church (Eph. 5:25) that He might unite His redeemed in the new covenant community of faith purchased by His sacrificial atonement. The church is a new body in which the risen Lord clothes Himself, being both its Head and animating Spirit (Eph. 1:23). Nurtured by the gifts of the Spirit bestowed on the church (1 Cor. 12:27-28; Rom. 12:6-8; Eph. 4:11-13) and bearing the fruit of the Spirit (Gal. 5:22-23), members of His body "attain to the unity of the faith and of the knowledge of the Son of God, to mature manhood, to the measure of the stature of the fulness of Christ" (Eph. 4:13), putting "on the new nature, created after the likeness of God in true righteousness and holiness" (Eph. 4:24). The church is God's chosen and ordained instrument through which He carries on His great work of redemption.

By Obedience to the Word of God

The power of God unto salvation is contained in the gospel (Rom. 1:16), God's good news of saving grace in Jesus Christ. He is the Word of life (1 John 1:1) by which we are born anew (1 Pet. 1:23) through the power of the Spirit (John 16:12-15; 1 Pet. 1:12). The Gospels were written that we might believe that "Jesus is the Christ, the Son of God, and that believing you may have life in His name" (John 20:31).

Salvation comes by believing the gospel preached to us. The Scriptures call us to decision. They direct us to put our faith in Christ the living Word who must not only be accepted as Savior but also obeyed as Lord. Though reconciled to God by faith (Rom. 1:17; 5:1), faith without works is dead (Jas. 2:17). The redeemed life is lived out in obedience to all Christ has commanded (Matt. 28:20). "Not every one who says to me, 'Lord, Lord,' shall enter the kingdom of heaven, but he who does the will of my Father who is in heaven" (Matt. 7:21). Obedience to Christ's words is like building a house on a rock-solid foundation against which the storms of life cannot prevail (Matt. 7:24-25).

The redeemed confirm their experience of salvation by carrying out the good works required of them. "For we are his workmanship, created in Christ Jesus for good works, which God prepared beforehand, that we should walk in them" (Eph. 2:10). By such obedience, one's salvation is worked out with "fear and trembling; for God is at work in you, both to will and to work for his good pleasure" (Phil. 2:12-13).

By receiving "with meekness the implanted word, which is able to save your souls," and by becoming a doer of the word and not a hearer only (Jas. 1:21-22), Christ is reverenced in our hearts as Lord (1 Pet. 3:15). By such obedience, the inspired Word of God fulfills its function as "profitable for teaching, for reproof, for correction, and for training in righteousness, that the man of God may be complete, equipped for every good work" (2 Tim. 3:16-17).

Through God's love poured into the heart by the Holy Spirit (Rom. 5:5), the redeemed give evidence that they belong to Christ and are obedient to His commandments (John 13:35; 14:15; 15:12,17). "If a man loves me, he will keep my word, and my Father will love him, and we will come to him and make our home with him" (John 14:23).

As all-sufficient for faith and practice, obedience to the Scriptures as the written Word of God is a sure measure of one's obedience to Christ, God's living and eternal Word of life.

Scripture As Revelation Unto Redemption

Everyone's Need of Redemption

Scripture makes plain that God has revealed Himself in order to redeem us. In the very beginning, it sets forth everyone's need of redemption (Gen. 3). The law, which is holy, just, and good, was given to reveal the nature of sin (Rom. 7:7-12).

The whole sweep of biblical history records God's initiative in seeking the redemption of His children. The Old Testament is the preparatory revelation for God's final and complete act of redemption in sending His only begotten Son as Savior of the world (John 3:16). The wonder and greatness of God's grace is seen in the fact that, while we were helpless sinners and enemies of God, by Christ's death He reconciles us to Himself (Rom. 5:6-11).

The Fulfillment of Revelation

The Scriptures not only record God's revealing/redemptive acts in history, reaching their climax in Jesus Christ, but speak also of a coming revelation in the end-time. Jesus often spoke of His return as the Son of man in judgment (Luke 17:30). As Lord of history, God is still at work moving the creation toward its culmination. Our present sufferings, therefore, are "not worth comparing with the glory that is to be revealed to us. For the creation waits with eager longing for the revealing of the sons of God . . . because the creation itself will be set free from its bondage to decay and obtain the glorious liberty of the children of God" (Rom. 8:18-21).

The New Testament contains the prophecy that God will create "new heavens and a new earth in which righteousness dwells" (2 Pet. 3:8-13; see Isa. 65:17). Until then, history continues as an act of God's forbearing grace, "not wishing that any should perish, but that all should reach repentance" (2 Pet. 3:9). The Book of Revelation, in vivid imagery and various figures of speech, depicts the final and absolute completion of God's purposes in creation and redemption. In Jesus Christ, God has already given us the key and clue by which He will judge and complete His eternal purpose (Rom. 2:16).

The Perfection of Our Redemption

The New Testament also speaks of the perfection of our redemption in the life and world to come. Such was the explicit promise of Jesus (John 14:1-6). The perfect revelation of God in glory brings with it the fullness of our salvation in Christ. God works all things together for good (Rom. 8:28) for those who live by the hope of the resurrection "to an inheritance which is imperishable, undefiled, and unfading, kept in heaven for you, who by God's power are guarded through faith for a salvation ready to be revealed in the last time" (1 Pet. 1:4-5; see 4:13; 5:1). Christ in the heart of the believer is his hope of the coming glory (Col. 1:27).

The final perfection of our redemption is the gift of the spiritual body of the resurrection (Rom. 8:23; 1 Cor. 15:44). "Beloved, we are God's children now; it does not yet appear what we shall be, but we know that when he appears we shall be like him, for we shall see him as he is" (1 John 3:2). The redeemed are destined to bear Christ's heavenly likeness forevermore (1 Cor. 15:49).

Epilogue

The Bible is God's own authoritative record of His revealing and redemptive acts in history. It discloses to us God's eternal purposes beginning with the account of creation and ending with the vivid prophecies of the consumation of all things. In the God-man, Jesus Christ, God revealed His character, power, and authority as Lord of nature and history. In Christ, God also reveals to us the person God destines us to be. Through the Bible's sacred pages, God calls us to repentance and offers us eternal life in Jesus Christ. To all who put their trust in Him, He gives "power to become children of God" (John 1:12).

As "the record of God's revelation of Himself to man" the Bible "is a perfect treasure of divine instruction"[3] making God known to us,

> That God, which ever lives and loves,
>   One God, one law, one element,
>   And one far-off divine event,
> To which the whole creation moves.[4]

Notes

1. William Least Heat Moon, *A Journey Into America: Blue Highways* (Boston: Little Brown & Company, 1982), p. 150.

2. From *The Works of Alfred Lord Tennyson* edited, with memoir by Hallam Lord Tennyson (New York: Macmillan, 1913).

3. *The Baptist Faith and Message,* (Nashville: The Sunday School Board, 1963), p. 7.

4. Tennyson, "In Memoriam."

Scripture Index